THE JOY OF
Cheesecake

DANA BOVBJERG & JEREMY IGGERS

BARRON'S

All inquiries should be addressed to:
Barron's Educational Series, Inc.
250 Wireless Boulevard
Hauppauge, New York 11788

Library of Congress Catalog Card No. 80-17014

Cloth Edition
International Standard Book No. 0-8120-5350-8

Paper Edition
International Standard Book No. 0-8120-4278-6

Library of Congress Cataloging in Publication Data

Bovbjerg, Dana
    The joy of cheesecake.
    Includes index.
    1. Cheesecake (Cookery)   I. Iggers, Jeremy,
joint author.   II. Title.
TX773.B67   641.8'653   80-17014
ISBN 0-8120-4278-6 (pbk)
ISBN 0-8120-5350-8

Credits:

Photography:
    Matthew Klein, color photographs
    Helen Feingold, food stylist
    Wonsook Kim, stylist

    table settings for Italian Cheesecake
    are from Ginori Fifth Avenue

Jacket and cover design: Milton Glaser, Inc.

Book design: Milton Glaser, Inc.
PRINTED IN HONG KONG

19 18 17 16 15 14 13 12 11

Contents

Preface

Although only two names appear on the cover, this book would not have been possible without the many people who gave us help and inspiration: Grandmother Bovbjerg, who taught Dana the joy of cheesecake by bringing it with her on the train when she came to visit from Chicago; Wilma Iggers, who taught her son to appreciate good food by feeding him lots of it; and, of course, the many people who were kind enough to share with us their kitchens, their recipes, and their cheese-cakes. Our special thanks to the people at the Sheepshead Café of Iowa City, Iowa, for letting Dana test his recipes on their clientele, and to Jim Basta and Gordon Johnson, for giving Jeremy his start in the cheesecake business. Finally we would like to thank our editor at Barron's, Carole Berglie, who put an enormous amount of time and effort into the project.

Introduction

*C*heesecakes are the most sensuous of desserts. After all, what pleasures hath the flesh to compare with a fresh slice of cheesecake and a hot cup of java? What mere carnal escapade can liken to the first bite of creamy white custard? Other confections may please, even delight the palate, but there is something special about cheesecake . . . something almost sinful in the richness of a well-made cheesecake . . . something that hints at the possibility of pleasure without limit. Cheesecake is excess. Perhaps it is that excess that arouses such strong passions. Forbidden fruit tastes best. You know, we know, everybody knows that each little bite of the stuff will add pounds to our bodies. Somewhere up in the sky a little cholesterol counter is going haywire, and we don't care. Not since the days of Adam and Eve has temptation had such a keen edge.

Ever since the dawn of time, mankind and womankind have striven to create the perfect cheesecake. It may well be the most noble struggle of the race. The earliest history of the art is lost in the shrouded eons of forgotten time, but we know that cheesecake was already a popular dish in ancient Greece. With the Roman conquest of Greece, the secret fell into Roman hands. The cheesecake recipe of the Roman soldier and statesman Cato survives to this day.

Place, on one side, two pounds of rye flour, which will serve to form the foundation, on which must be placed biscuits, formed of crisp paste; on the other, put four pounds of wheat, and two pounds of alica [grains of fine wheat, stripped of their husks and crushed; to which was added, in order to whiten them, a peculiar

kind of chalk found between Naples and Pozzouli]. This latter must be left to infuse in water, and, when well soaked, it must be thrown into a treading trough, and well worked with the hand. You then mix with it the four pounds of wheat flour, in order to make the whole into biscuits, or dry marchpans. This paste must be worked in a basket, and as it dries, each separate marchpan must be shaped. When they have acquired a convenient form, rub them on all sides with a piece of stuff soaked in oil, and the same must be done to the foundation of the placenta before placing the marchpans on it. During these preparations, make the hearth very hot, as well as the cover of the tart dish intended to cook it. Then spread the two pounds of rye flour you have in reserve over fourteen pounds of cheese of sheep's milk. Make of this a light paste for the foundation already mentioned. This cheese ought to be very fresh, and previously soaked in three waters. It is allowed to drain slowly between the hands, and when it has been left to dry, it is kneaded. Take a flour sieve, and pass the cheese through it before mixing with the rye. Then add four pounds and a half of good honey; mix well; place the foundation furnished with its band, on a board a foot square, covered with bay leaves rubbed with oil, and form the placenta. Begin by covering the whole of the base with a layer of marchpans, which you place one after the other, and cover slightly with cheese mixed with honey. Finally, you arrange the marchpans on the foundation, and prepare the hearth to a moderate degree of heat; place the placenta on it; cover it with the tart dish cover already heated, and spread live charcoal underneath and all around. The cooking must be done very slowly, *and as soon as the pie is taken from the hearth, it must be rubbed with honey.**

Of course, unless you know where to get fourteen pounds of sheep's cheese, it isn't going to do you a whole lot of good.

We may speculate that cheesecake was first introduced to Great Britain and Western Europe by the Roman conquests. All across Europe, it developed in a multitude of forms. In Russia, cheesecakes became an Easter tradition of the Orthodox Church. By the time of the Renaissance, cheesecakes were flourishing. In his diary entry of August 11, 1667, Samuel Pepys savors the memory of "some of the best cheesecakes that ever I [ate] in my life." The Golden Age of Cheesecakes came in the years that followed. By the time Mrs. Hannah Glasse published her *Art of Cookery* in 1747, the cheesecake repertoire included saffron cheesecakes, lemon cheesecakes, and many more. In 1872, American dairymen achieved a technological breakthrough that ushered in the Modern Age of Cheesecakes. In attempting to duplicate the popular neufchâtel cheese of France, they hit upon a formula for an unripened cheese that was even richer and creamier than neufchâtel. They named it cream cheese. The rest is, as they say, history.

By now, there are more different kinds of cheesecakes than crumbs in a graham cracker crust. You have no idea how many different kinds. When we started collecting recipes, we had no idea. Every little country in Europe big enough to sell postage stamps has its own cheesecake. Everybody's Aunt Hilda has a recipe tucked away. Pineapple cheesecakes. Chocolate cheesecakes. Pumpkin

*CATO, DE RE RUSTICA, FROM THE PANTROPHEON, OR A HISTORY OF FOOD AND ITS PREPARATION IN ANCIENT TIMES, BY ALEXIS SOYER, 1853, REPRINTED BY THE PADDINGTON PRESS, COPYRIGHT 1977, PP. 287–288.

5

cheesecakes. Peanut butter and jelly cheesecakes. Tofu cheesecakes. You name it.

The popularity of cheesecake has grown tremendously over the years, but for many people a love affair with cheesecake is at best a bittersweet romance. Since they do not know how to make cheesecake for themselves, they are forever at the mercy of restaurant chefs or even worse, supermarket freezer cases. This book can put an end to all that. In the privacy of your own kitchen you can learn to make cheesecake as good as you will find in the best restaurants, and far better than you could find in a freezer case.

Perhaps you have been held back by the notion that anything that tastes so good must be awfully difficult to make. Cheesefeathers! Most cheesecakes are really quite easy to make. There are a few basic techniques you have to learn, but even these are simple, and if you follow instructions carefully you should create a superb cheesecake the first time you try.

Of course, to fully experience the joy of cheesecake, you must go beyond mere technique. Indeed, many times beginning bakers get so wrapped up in worrying about whether they are "doing it right" that they can't actually enjoy what they are doing. The possibilities for cheesecake creativity are as rich as your imagination. Once you've tried your hand at some of our recipes, you may well be able to surpass them with a cheesecake of your own. By varying ingredients, proportions, and baking times, you can produce a cheesecake that is heavy or light, moist or dry, cakelike or smooth, according to your mood. We wrote the chapters on ingredients and techniques to be aids to your improvisation. Explore!

Cheese and Other Ingredients

Kilimanjaro Cheesecake

$\mathscr{T}$he ingredients are, of course, what make one cheesecake different from another. The following is a brief discussion of the major ingredients for the cheesecakes in this book, along with some suggestions that may inspire you to try other ingredients for your own cheesecake creativity.

Cheese

The most essential ingredient in any cheesecake is — you guessed it — cheese. The cheeses most commonly used are cream cheese, neufchâtel, cottage cheese, and ricotta, but some of the recipes also use such cheeses as gouda and swiss.

Cheese is made from milk, whether it be from cows, goats, or sheep. It has even been made from buffalo and reindeer milk. The milk is separated into curds (solids) and whey (liquids), and most cheese is made from the curds, although ricotta is produced from the whey. The fresh, or uncured, cheeses are the ones you mostly will be using in your cheesecakes, and these include cream cheese, neufchâtel, and cottage cheese. Although these unripened cheeses all have roughly the same proportion of cheese solids (roughly 15 to 18 percent), they differ greatly in their butterfat content. All other things being equal, the higher the butterfat content, the creamier the cheesecake.

CREAM CHEESE:

Cream cheese, made from milk, must contain at least 33 percent butterfat, and has one hundred calories per ounce. The water content is 50 percent, the texture is smooth and soft, the flavor delicate. Allow the cheese to come to room temperature before using it so that it will blend easily with other ingredients.

Cream cheese is sold in three-ounce and eight-ounce packages in all supermarkets. Packages are usually dated, so be sure to check for freshness when you purchase. Once purchased, the cheese is usable for at least three weeks, sometimes even longer. The most widely distributed brand is Kraft's Philadelphia Brand Cream Cheese, although store brands are also available. We've found that these store brands vary somewhat in quality; they aren't always as smooth and rich as we'd like. You may want to do some experimenting to see how well store brands available in your area compare in flavor and texture with the national brand. Imitation cream cheese is available in places, but we don't recommend it for your cheesecakes.

NEUFCHÂTEL:

Neufchâtel made in the United States is very similar to cream cheese. It is made from whole or skim milk, or a combination of milk and cream. Its butterfat content is a little lower — about 23 percent — and it usually has about seventy calories per ounce. The water content is 60 percent; the texture is a little lighter than cream cheese. The flavor is milder, but in most cases it can be substituted for cream cheese when a lower fat content is desired. But then again, who do you think you're kidding? No matter how you slice it, cheesecake is fattening. If you do decide to adapt a cream-cheese recipe for use with neufchâtel, remember that the water content is a little higher than cream cheese; you may want to increase slightly the quantity of one of the moisture-holding ingredients (such as flour, cornstarch, gelatin, or egg whites) called for in the recipe.

Neufchâtel is sold much as is cream cheese and the usable life is about the same. Do not confuse this with the French neufchâtel, which is similar to a camembert.

COTTAGE CHEESE:

A wide variety of cottage cheeses are available on the market, ranging in butterfat content from ½ percent to 4 percent. The dry-curd cottage cheeses have roughly twenty calories per ounce, those with 4 percent butterfat contain about thirty calories per ounce. The curds themselves are made from skim milk. The richer cottage cheeses, sometimes called creamed cottage cheese, are made by adding whole milk and cream to the curds. Unless otherwise noted, our recipes call for the use of creamed cottage cheese (at least 2 percent butterfat) carefully drained of excess moisture.

FARMER CHEESE:

This is skim-milk cottage cheese that has been pressed into small squares or rectangles. It is usually sold in delicatessens or specialty shops as bricks. Dry-curd cottage cheese can be substituted for farmer cheese if necessary.

RICOTTA:

In the United States, ricotta is almost always made from whole milk or a combination of milk and whey. The fat

content is from 4 to 10 percent and there are about fifty calories per ounce. The water content is about 72 percent; the texture is slightly grainy, ranging to creamier if made from all milk. It is sold in fifteen- or thirty-two-ounce containers, which are usually dated. Be sure to check for freshness, since this cheese keeps only for a few days.

Skim-milk ricotta is also available, and this resembles more the original ricotta made in Italy. Our recipes call for whole-milk ricotta.

CURED CHEESES:

The recipes in this book also use blue cheese, gouda, feta, and swiss cheese. These are ripened cheeses, made from the curds and aged.

Cream

Many of the recipes call for cream, either sweet or sour. Usually the cream is added to lighten the cake or to provide a richer flavor.

SWEET CREAM:

Cream comes in several different grades, depending upon the fat content. Heavy cream contains about 40 percent butterfat, 5 percent milk solids, and over 50 percent water. It has about fifty-three calories per tablespoon. Light cream contains about 20 percent butterfat and 7 percent milk solids; the rest is water. It has about thirty-two calories per tablespoon. Half-and-half, a blending of heavy cream and milk, has about 12 percent butterfat, 7 percent milk solids, and 51 percent water. It has about twenty calories per tablespoon.

Heavy cream is added to the ingredients of a cheesecake most often as whipped cream. When whipped, heavy cream will double in volume; for best results, use a chilled bowl and chilled beaters. Often confectioners' sugar is added as the cream begins to stiffen to help retain the volume. Heavy cream is perishable, so buy only as much as you plan to use within the next few days. A new, ultrapasteurized type of cream is now widely available which has a much longer life. Many people find that it does not whip up as high and that it lacks much of the flavor of the more traditional kind. We leave the choice to you.

Light cream is used less often in baking but is available in most supermarkets. It also is very perishable and should be purchased in small quantities. In the recipes included in this book, we have indicated that half-and-half may be substituted. Half-and-half is also available in most supermarkets, but you can mix up your own from equal quantities of whole milk and heavy cream.

SOUR CREAM:

This is cream that has been processed commercially so as to be soured under ideal conditions. It contains about 20 percent butterfat, about 7 percent milk solids, and the remainder is water. There are about thirty calories per tablespoon. Sour cream is sold in containers varying from one-half pound to one pound. It is usually dated, so check for freshness when you purchase the container. Sour cream will last up to two weeks in the refrigerator. Most brands seem to be uniformly good.

Sugar and Other Sweeteners

Every dessert cheesecake requires a sweetening of some kind. Most of the recipes in this book use granulated sugar. However, it is possible to substitute brown sugar or honey in almost all of the recipes.

HONEY:

Remember that honey will make your cheesecake darker, which you may find undesirable. And, since it is less soluble than granulated sugar, it is necessary to be especially careful that it is blended into the cheese mixture. Honey is used as the sweetener in the Yogurt No-Bake Cheesecake and the No-Bake Honey Cheese Pie, but if you want to use it in other cakes, you must adjust the quantities. Since honey is sweeter and has a higher moisture content than granulated sugar, use one-third less honey by volume and, when possible, reduce the volume of other liquids by one-fourth cup for each cup of honey used. This can be done by appropriately varying the proportions of dry (cream cheese) and moist (sour cream) dairy products.

BROWN SUGAR:

This is fine crystals of sugar coated with molasses, sold in either a dark or light form. Brown sugar is used as an ingredient in the Praline Cheesecake, but could be substituted for granulated sugar in other cakes as well. As with honey, brown sugar will make your cake darker, and you must blend it in well. Measurements will remain the same. We don't recommend using the granulated brown sugar or the liquid form of brown sugar.

CONFECTIONERS' SUGAR:

Also commonly available, this sugar has been crushed to a powder similar in texture to cornstarch. It is used in cheesecakes primarily in beating egg whites, as a means of stiffening them. Often it is also added to whipped cream as a sweetening.

Flour and Other Thickening Agents

Although eggs are generally best for holding together the ingredients of a successful cheesecake, there are several other ingredients that can be used in addition or in place of them. Flour and cornstarch also thicken the batter and stabilize the moisture content.

FLOUR:

In our recipes, we indicate either all-purpose flour or self-rising flour. The all-purpose flour can be either bleached or unbleached, and today usually comes pre-sifted. If not, sift before measuring. Self-rising flour is bleached flour to which has been added a leavening agent such as baking powder. Whichever you use, remember to use it judiciously. Too much flour will make the cheesecake tough.

CORNSTARCH:

Finer than flour, cornstarch is more effective as a thickening agent. As with flour, too much cornstarch will leave your cake tough.

GELATIN:

Unflavored gelatin is commonly available in one-ounce envelopes. It is a thickening agent that works best when refrigerated, thus this is the basic ingredient in most of the no-bake cakes. It must be blended well with the ingredients and completely dissolved. Too much gelatin will make a rubbery cheesecake.

Milk and Milk Products

Milk is used infrequently in cheesecakes. In this book we use milk in the Custard Cheesecake, and for that we recommend whole milk. The Low-Calorie Cheesecake does include a small quantity of skim milk.

Other milk products that appear more frequently in cheesecakes are buttermilk, sweetened condensed milk, and yogurt. Buttermilk is made when special bacteria are added to lowfat milk; therefore, an average eight-ounce serving has about one hundred calories. It is available in most supermarkets, in one-quart containers.

Sweetened condensed milk is evaporated milk to which sugar has been added. It is very high in calories — about 980 calories in a cup. It is sold, unrefrigerated, in most supermarkets.

Yogurt is milk that has been allowed to ferment to a semisolid consistency. It can be made from either whole or skim milk. It is often used as a substitute for sour cream, since it often achieves a similar result. If you do attempt to substitute yogurt for sour cream, use whole milk yogurt if possible and drain carefully of excess water. Yogurt has far fewer calories as well — about 120, as opposed to sour cream's average of 475 per cup. Yogurt is sold in all supermarkets in eight-ounce and larger containers. You can also make it at home quite easily.

Eggs

Since the cheeses and creams used in cheesecakes have such a high moisture content, it is necessary to have an ingredient that can hold or absorb water. The most popular and most elegant solution to this problem is the egg. Also, since egg yolks and whites harden as they bake, they add body and texture to the cheesecake. Egg yolks in particular contain lecithin, an emulsifier, which has the effect of congealing the fats in the cheeses. Generally a cheesecake recipe with a high fat content will also call for relatively more eggs.

EGG WHITES:

Many recipes require you to separate the eggs and to beat the whites until they form stiff peaks with the beaters of your mixer. As egg whites are beaten, the albumen is spun out into a finer and finer web of protein; the finer the structure, the more moisture the batter can hold. If the whites are overbeaten or overheated, however, this delicate structure collapses and the result is a soggy cheesecake. Since air is also encapsulated, the egg whites also add lightness to the cake. Oddly enough, the freshest eggs are not the best for cheesecakes; the whites of eggs that are a few days old can be beaten to a larger volume.

Unless you have access to farm-fresh eggs, though, this isn't likely to be a problem; most store-bought eggs are already at least several days old.

When beating the egg whites, add a dash of cream of tartar to make them more stable. To make the whites stiffer (if this is desired), you can blend in some confectioners' sugar or a boiling sugar syrup once the whites have reached the soft-peak stage.

Butter and Shortening

Except for a few of the special cheesecakes, butter is not found among the ingredients in the fillings. However, it is basic for most of the crusts. We recommend using sweet butter, not salted.

Some of the individual crust recipes offer margarine as a suitable substitute. Shortening, a major ingredient for the Basic Pastry Pie Crust, makes a flakier crust than butter.

Fruits and Nuts

Many of the recipes use the grated rind of a lemon or orange. For best results, we greatly prefer the fresh peel to the dried; as the peels dry they lose much of their aromatic oils. The only part of the peel that is used is the outermost, colored layer, called the zest. The zest can be removed with a zester or with any ordinary grater.

Many of our recipes also call for small amounts of lemon juice. We're partial to freshly squeezed lemons, but we've also had good results with reconstituted lemon juice. You may wish to experiment, varying the amount to suit your taste.

Nuts are used in a number of recipes, oftentimes ground fine. For best results, we find that a light toasting brings out the flavor in almonds and hazelnuts (filberts) and that toasted nuts retain more of their crunch when used in the batter. To toast the nuts, spread them on a baking pan and bake for ten minutes or so in a 350-degree oven, stirring occasionally to ensure even browning. If you use hazelnuts that still have their paperlike skins, the skins must be removed before use — they acquire a burnt taste during toasting.

The cost of some nuts, especially walnuts, in small quantities is pretty outrageous, but you can save quite a bit by buying them in bulk. Shelled nuts turn rancid fairly quickly, though, so we recommend storing them in the refrigerator or freezer, well wrapped.

Spices and Flavorings

Spices such as cinnamon, cloves, ginger, nutmeg, and cardamom appear frequently in the recipes because they contrast so well with the mildness of the cheeses. Spices do deteriorate as they sit on your rack, so be sure to always have fresh ones on hand for your cheesecakes. Cinnamon and ginger can be used ground commercially, but you may want to grate your own nutmeg and grind

your own cloves or cardamom from the whole spices. We have found a coffee grinder to be a very effective device for accomplishing this.

Certain flavorings are used in the book, including the commonly available vanilla extract or instant-coffee powder, but also rosewater, a medieval ingredient again appearing on the shelves of specialty stores. You can also find it in drugstores.

Chocolate is used in the mocha-flavored and chocolate-flavored cheesecakes. We recommend using the real baking chocolate sold in most stores — either semisweet or unsweetened, depending upon the recipe.

A Word About Equipment

$\mathcal{O}$f course, all you really need to make a cheesecake is a mixing bowl, a whisk, a mixing spoon, and a baking pan. But today's cooks are usually well equipped, so we will discuss some of those items that are helpful to have.

Electric Appliances

MIXER:

A mixer is handy to make the cream cheese smooth and light, and you can also whip the cream or beat the egg whites. Use a large mixing bowl when blending major ingredients to allow enough air space to give the beaters a chance. You will find that the cheese will blend better if worked at room temperature or warmed for five minutes in the oven at 250 degrees.

When beating egg whites, remember that your beaters and bowl must be free of butter or oil and there should be no bits of yolk on them. If you are whipping cream, you'll have more success with a chilled bowl and beaters.

BLENDER:

The only use you will probably make of your blender in preparing cheesecakes is that of breaking up cookies or crackers for crumbs. How to do this is described along with the recipe for the Basic Crumb Crust.

PROCESSOR:

A food processor comes in handy for whipping cream cheese, chopping nuts, making graham cracker crumbs, or blending cottage cheese to a smooth consistency. It cannot

be used to beat egg whites or whip cream, though, as it will not incorporate air. Be careful not to overdo it when using the processor — you don't want cracker flour or powdered nuts.

Bowls and Utensils

MIXING BOWLS:

When we indicate in the recipes to use a large mixing bowl, we are suggesting one about twelve inches in diameter. The cakes in this book tend to be large — nine inches on the average — and this means that you will be working with up to two pounds of cheese, some eggs, and so forth.

If you prefer to beat your egg whites by hand, you will get the very best results if you use a copper bowl and a wire whisk. Second best would be a bowl with a broad bottom. You want to provide enough air around the whites as you beat so that the air can be incorporated into the eggs.

SIEVE:

The sieve serves a double purpose. It can be used to drain cottage cheese and also to smooth the curds to a finer consistency. Place the cottage cheese in the sieve, allow the liquid to drain out, and then with a spoon or spatula, force the curds through the holes. The result should have a consistency somewhat like ricotta. Sieves are available in most stores that sell kitchen equipment, but you can substitute a common kitchen strainer or even a colander with very small holes.

Pineapple Cheesecake

PASTRY BLENDER:

To make the Basic Pastry Pie Crust, we suggest you get a good pastry blender. This handy device will help you incorporate the butter with the flour for a nice, coarse-meal texture.

RUBBER SPATULA:

Just about every cook who bakes has one of these handy items. They allow you to scrape all the batter out of the pan. They are also useful in smoothing the top of the filling before baking the cake.

Pots and Pans

DOUBLE BOILER:

This is a handy kitchen item you can use to melt chocolate for the chocolate and mocha cheesecakes, as well as to gently heat egg yolks or to dissolve gelatin. The double boiler is the best way to control the heat when working with delicate ingredients.

BAKING PAN:

There are several important differences between cheesecakes and flour-based cakes. The most significant of these is the fact that you can't remove a cheesecake from the pan by turning it upside-down. Unless you plan to serve the cheesecake in the pan you bake it in (as in the case of many of the cheese pies), you are best advised to use a springform pan. These are round baking pans, made of aluminum or tinplate, with an expandable collar and a removable bottom. False-bottomed pans are also excellent

for this purpose, but they are rather difficult to come by these days.

Unless otherwise specified, the recipes in this collection call for a nine-inch springform pan. To be on the safe side, it is best to use pans with a high (three-inch) collar, as the tallest cakes will likely pour over the sides of the lower pans as they bake in the oven. For more hints on using springform pans, see the special article by Pierre Franey, of the *New York Times*.

The cheese pies are best made in common pie pans, made usually of glass, aluminum, or aluminum foil. There are a few cheesecakes in this book that use rectangular baking dishes, such as are used for lasagne.

OVENS:

Our recipes should work equally well in gas or electric ovens. Accurate baking temperatures are important, though, and unfortunately many ovens, especially older ones, are quite inaccurate. If in doubt, test your oven with an oven thermometer and adjust settings appropriately.

Convection ovens are ideal for baking cheesecakes because they distribute heat evenly throughout the oven. As a general rule, you can adjust baking recipes for convection ovens by reducing the recommended temperature by twenty-five to fifty degrees and the recommended baking time by 20 to 30 percent. This is only an approximation, though; the best way to judge when a cheesecake is done is by appearance. The cake is ready when the top appears firm at the center and has just begun to brown.

SPRINGFORM CAKE PAN

When I was young I regarded making a cheesecake as a riskier business than it seems to me now. The primary source of the relative calm I feel today is not the passage of time or the accumulation of skills — although they've helped — but the springform pan, a tool whose acquaintance I made for the first time when I became a chef in this country after years of cooking in France.

A cheesecake, like an ice cream cake and some other kinds of pastry, does not give you the opportunity to cover up mistakes with a delicate glaze or a dense frosting. The walls of the cake remain unadorned, so if the cake has adhered to the side of the pan because of inadequate preparation before the batter was poured into the mold, the cheesecake will emerge blotched, perhaps torn, and will stand there on its pedestal as if the elevation were meant as a mockery.

The extrication of a cheesecake from its mold is made the harder by the fact that cheesecake is not meant to be placed upside down as are cakes that take an icing, so it can't be turned out of a pan in one motion. The springform pan greatly diminishes the amount of risky manipulation required. While the cake bakes, the pan wall is held tightly closed by a clip. When it is done, the clip is opened, allowing the walls of the mold to spring into an expanded position, pulling away from the cake. The wall is then lifted up and away.

Although this is simple to do, the springform still requires diligent preparation. The wall and the bottom should be well greased. The best way to do that is to melt butter and chill the pan at the same time. Then brush the warm butter onto the cold metal. It will go on smoothly and evenly, congealing as it does, so that it won't drip.

This careful application is important both to prevent sticking when the cake is removed and to allow all kinds of cakes to rise uniformly (a sticking spot on the wall will tug at the cake as it tries to rise).

If the recipe calls for a flouring of the mold, that should be done uniformly, too. Don't sprinkle the flour on. Rather place a half cup or so of flour into the pan and toss it around until it has adhered everywhere on the surface, then turn the pan upside down and strike it gently to remove the excess.

Springform pans come in a number of sizes. Those in the Kaiser brand — a widely available line of plated-steel molds that have waffled bottoms to add the strength necessary in moving heavy cakes — come in diameters of eight, eight and a half and nine and a half inches.

The size variation is useful because some cakes are fine the second day while others — notably the cheese and ice cream ones — don't last well. So it is often prudent to make an especially small cake such as the eight-inch one.

Springform pans cost in the vicinity of $5. They are sometimes sold with interchangeable bottoms that will produce ring-shaped cakes and thus add to the pan's versatility. — *Pierre Franey*

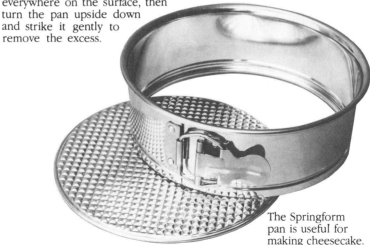

The Springform pan is useful for making cheesecake.

Some Practical Tips

Modifying the Recipes

Cheesecakes are rich desserts. Depending upon the rest of your meal and upon your guests' appetites, the nine-inch cakes in this book will serve an average of from ten to sixteen people. However, it is conceivable that you might want to make a smaller or larger cake, based on the same ingredients. To modify the recipes for use in an eight- or ten-inch pan, decrease or increase the quantities by approximately one-fifth.

Leftovers

Cheesecakes are just as good the next day, but they should be refrigerated. To keep the cake from drying out or absorbing refrigerator odors, wrap the cake or keep it in a closed container. If it is difficult to wrap the cake directly without marring the surface, we recommend returning the cake to the pan and covering the pan with plastic wrap or foil.

Freezing for Future Use

Some cheesecakes freeze better than others. The rich, heavy cream-cheese cakes freeze well, while lighter and moister custardy cakes freeze less well. We do not recommend freezing cottage-cheese cakes. Refrigerate the cake before you freeze it and wrap it carefully to prevent freezer burn.

Cheesecakes as Gifts

Bakers who make cheesecakes or cheese pies to give away as gifts face the problem of perhaps never seeing their pans again. On the other hand, if you try to remove the cheesecake from the metal bottom, you run the risk of damaging the cake in the process. Here's our solution. If you are making cakes, obtain a supply of nine-inch cardboard pizza disks. If you can't find these in the housewares department of your local department store, try to find a pizzeria that makes nine-inch pies or make the pie disks yourself from sturdy cardboard. Wrap the disks in foil — they will get soggy otherwise — and use them in place of the metal bottom. If you are making pies, then simply obtain the packaged aluminum pie pans. They come in several different sizes and are disposable.

Cutting the Cake

Here is the best-kept secret of the trade: dental floss. It is just about impossible to cut a cheesecake cleanly with a knife; too much of the precious filling sticks to the sides of the blade. You can lick this problem by taking a long strand of dental floss, stretching it taut, and gently pressing it through the cake. Don't try to pull the floss back up through the cut you have made; simply pull it out when you reach the bottom. Either waxed or unwaxed floss may be used, but do avoid mint-flavored. This method works well on cakes with crumb crusts. With harder crusts, you may want to finish off with a thin, sharp knife.

Conversion Factors

The following are conversion tables and other informational items applicable to those converting the recipes in this book for use in other English-speaking countries. The cup and spoon measures given in this book are U.S. Customary; use these tables when working with British Imperial or metric kitchen utensils.

Liquid Measures

The old Imperial pint is larger than the U.S. pint; therefore note the following when measuring liquid ingredients:

U.S.

1 cup = 8 fluid ounces
½ cup = 4 fluid ounces
1 tablespoon = ¾ fluid ounce

Imperial

1 cup = 10 fluid ounces
½ cup = 5 fluid ounces
1 tablespoon = 1 fluid ounce

U.S. Measure	Metric	Imperial*
1 quart	946 ml	1½ + pints
1 pint	473 ml	¾ + pint
1 cup	236 ml	− ½ pint
1 tablespoon	15 ml	−1 tablespoon
1 teaspoon	5 ml	−1 teaspoon

*Note that exact quantities cannot always be given. Differences are more crucial when dealing with larger quantities. For teaspoon and tablespoon measures, simply use scant quantities, or for more accurate conversions rely upon metric measures.

Weight and Volume Measures

U.S. cooking procedures usually measure certain items by volume, although in the Metric or Imperial systems they are measured by weight. Here are some approximate equivalents for basic items appearing in this book.*

	U.S. Customary	Metric	Imperial
Butter	1 cup	250 g	8 ounces
	½ cup	125 g	4 ounces
	¼ cup	62 g	2 ounces
	1 tablespoon	15 g	½ ounce
Cornstarch	1 teaspoon	10 g	⅓ ounce
Cream of Tartar	1 teaspoon	3-4 g	⅛ ounce
Flour (sifted all-purpose)	1 cup	128 g	4¼ ounces
	½ cup	60 g	2⅛ ounces
	¼ cup	32 g	1 ounce
Nut Meats	1 cup	112 g	4 ounces
Raisins (or Sultanas)	¾ cup	125 g	4 ounces
Sugar: Granulated (Caster)	1 cup	240 g	8 ounces
	½ cup	120 g	4 ounces
	¼ cup	60 g	2 ounces
	1 tablespoon	15 g	½ ounce

(continued)

*So as to avoid awkward measurements, some conversions are not exact.

	U.S. Customary	Metric	Imperial
Confectioners' (Icing)	1 cup	140 g	5 ounces
	½ cup	70 g	3 ounces
	¼ cup	35 g	1+ ounce
	1 tablespoon	10 g	¼ ounce
Brown	1 cup	160 g	5⅓ ounces
	½ cup	80 g	2⅔ ounces
	¼ cup	40 g	1⅓ ounces
	1 tablespoon	10 g	⅓ ounce

Oven Temperatures

Gas Mark	¼	2	4	6	8
Fahrenheit	225	300	350	400	450
Centigrade	107	150	178	205	233

Miscellaneous

To help you substitute ingredients with approximately the same composition as intended for the recipes, note the following:

Cream

Heavy Cream = 40% butterfat. Substitute Whipping Cream or Double Cream.

Light Cream = 20% butterfat. Substitute Sterilised Cream or Single Cream.

Half and Half = 12% butterfat. Substitute Sterilised Half Cream or Half Cream.

Other

Cream Cheese = Full Fat Soft Cheese (20-45% butterfat)
Granulated Sugar = Caster Sugar
Whole-Wheat Flour = Wheatmeal Flour
Vanilla Extract = Vanilla Essence

Some Basic Techniques

$\mathcal{C}$heesecakes are not nearly as difficult to prepare as is commonly believed, and if you follow the steps in the recipes, you should have little difficulty producing a perfect cheesecake the first time you try. However, there are a few pointers that should be kept in mind, in dealing with both the crusts and the fillings.

Making the Crusts

The techniques for preparing the crusts are described on pages 43 to 63. We have recommended crusts to go with each of our recipes, but keep in mind that these are only our suggestions. Do a little experimenting and see if you come up with a combination that you like better.

The Fillings

Before you start, make sure that you have all ingredients ready and at hand. If at all possible, allow the cream cheese and eggs to reach room temperature; the egg whites can then be beaten to a larger volume and the cream cheese will blend much more easily with the other ingredients. This process can be hastened by putting the cheese in a warm oven (100 to 200 degrees) for a few minutes before using.

In blending the batter, start with the dry ingredients first — flour, baking powder, salt — and combine these. Flour or cornstarch must be thoroughly sifted (or pressed against the spoon with your finger) to remove lumps before adding it to the batter.

When mixing the cheese and eggs, make sure that they are completely blended and smooth before adding the flavorings, sour cream, or heavy cream. Once the batter has been thinned out by the addition of these ingredients, it becomes impossible to remove any lumps, so take care.

In general, all ingredients except the egg whites, whipped cream, or sour cream should be added slowly and beaten until completely smooth. Egg whites and whipped cream should be folded in very gently, so as not to lose the air put into them through the whipping.

Beaten egg whites are the only delicate part of a cheesecake. Under ideal conditions they can be beaten safely to two to four times their initial volume, but contact with grease or fat in any form will prevent that. It is important that the eggs be separated carefully; any trace of yolk that remains in the whites should be scooped out or drawn out with a moist cloth or paper towel. When beating the whites, start slowly and gradually increase speed, beating continuously until soft peaks are formed. It is possible to beat the whites to an even greater volume and firmness, but often this is not advisable; they will be more fragile and more likely to break down during baking. To ensure even beating, vary the depth and position of the beaters. Blenders and food processors are not suitable for beating egg whites or whipping cream, as they will not allow the eggs to incorporate the proper volume of air. For the same reason, the beaters must be only partially immersed in the whites (no problem when making a single cheesecake).

If you beat the egg whites too long, their structure will collapse and the whites will begin to reliquify. At this point, all is lost; they will not rise again. Sneak them into an omelette, mash them in with the dog chow, or use them in a pommade for your hair if you like, but do not try to use them in a cheesecake. Start over.

It is not possible to blend beaten egg whites or whipped cream into a batter with a mixer without destroying much of their lightness in the process. They must be folded in by hand with a large spoon or whisk, using a gentle scooping motion to draw them to the bottom on the bowl. Once they have been incorporated, the batter should be poured gently into the pan and placed in the preheated oven immediately.

Baking

Since each oven seems to have its own set of idiosyncrasies, it is impossible to provide temperatures and baking times that will be ideal for all. The temperatures and times we have recommended should be appropriate under most conditions. If you are in doubt about your oven, it is safest to use a slightly lower temperature than the one recommended and to allow the cake to bake a little longer.

The best test of when a cheesecake is done is its appearance. The sides should be raised and just barely beginning to brown. The center may still be a little soft at this point, but it will harden as the cake cools. When the cake reaches this stage, turn the oven off. If possible, allow the cheesecake to cool in the oven, with the oven door slightly open (a wooden spoon accomplishes the job

nicely). If this is not possible, the cheesecake may be cooled on a rack.

Cooling

Once the cake has reached room temperature, refrigerate it for at least four hours before serving. To best do this, cover the cake, still in the pan, with a layer of foil or plastic wrap drawn tightly over the top to seal out odors and prevent drying out. Place the cake on a middle or upper shelf of the refrigerator.

Troubleshooting

The most common disaster that beginning cheesecake bakers encounter is cracking. If the egg whites were beaten and folded properly, then the problem is probably in the baking and cooling. As the cheescake bakes, it gives off a considerable amount of moisture. If it gives off too much or gives it off too fast, the cake will crack. One solution to this problem is to increase the humidity of the oven.

Some commercial bakeries have steam injection systems designed for this purpose. At home this same result can be obtained by placing the cake pan in a water bath or by placing a pan of water on the bottom shelf of the oven. Since springform pans are not watertight, it is advisable to place a skirt of aluminum foil around the entire bottom of the pan before placing it in a water bath.

Deep concentric cracks and a dark brown top indicate that the cake was baked too long and/or at too high a temperature. Such cracks are usually indicative of extensive damage to the egg white structure and consequently mean a soggy cheesecake. Don't serve it to company.

Grand Canyon crevices across the center of the cheesecake are unsightly, but usually not very serious. They are often caused by drafts or come about during the cooling process. Two safeguards can be recommended. Do not open the oven any more or any longer than is absolutely necessary. Unless the recipe specifically calls for it, never open the door during the first thirty minutes of baking.

To prevent cracking during the cooling process, run a knife or spatula along the edge of the pan so that the cake can pull away freely as it contracts. Don't forget that unsightly cracks can be hidden with judicious use of a topping.

By and large, the same hints apply to all varieties of cheesecakes, but a few points should be kept in mind. Cheese pies and cheesecakes prepared without separately beaten egg whites can be baked at somewhat higher temperatures. In recipes that call for the use of gelatin, the gelatin should be allowed to thicken, but not set before it is added to the batter. If it should set, place the bowl in hot water until it reliquifies. It may then be cooled again until it reaches the desired consistency.

The Pie Crusts

*S*ome cheesecake purists insist that a crust is an unnecessary distraction from the true pleasures of cheesecake gastronomy. Indeed, we include a recipe for the Barebottom Cheesecake. But even if you are of this persuasion, you will undoubtedly find that a light dusting of graham cracker crumbs into a lightly buttered baking pan will greatly facilitate removing the finished cheesecake.

We include twelve suggested crusts, the last one being a simple dusting. In addition, we indicate some variations upon those basic crusts that give you even greater options.

Basic Crumb Crust

YIELDS:
ONE 9-INCH CRUST

This is one of the most popular crusts for cheesecakes because it is quick and easy. Nearly any kind of cracker or biscuit can be made into crumbs, and it is the type of crumbs you choose that also determines any additional flavorings you may want to add.

You can buy unflavored bread crumbs or graham cracker crumbs readymade in any supermarket, but if you decide to use any other type, then you will have to make the crumbs yourself. There are as many ways of making crumbs as there are crumbers crushing. The easiest way is to place the crackers, cookies, or whatever you are using, a few pieces at a time, into the container of a blender or food processor. Run the motor briefly until the crumbs are small and uniform.

Another way is to place the crackers in a sturdy plastic bag and roll the bag on a bread board with a rolling pin. This works well and also satisfies certain atavistic urges that might otherwise be expressed in less socially acceptable ways. In any event, remember that you want crumbs, not flour.

Prebaked crusts are crisper than chilled ones; this is important if the crumbs are a bit soggy.

INGREDIENTS:
1½ CUPS GRAHAM CRACKER
   CRUMBS
6 TABLESPOONS BUTTER,
   MELTED
¼ CUP GRANULATED SUGAR

1 If you are prebaking the shell, preheat the oven to 350 degrees.

2 Place the crumbs in a mixing bowl and add the butter and sugar. Blend well.

3 Press the crumb mixture onto the bottom and partly up the sides of a greased 9-inch baking dish, pie pan, or springform mold. Smooth the crumb mixture along the bottom to an even thickness.

4 Chill the crust for 5 to 10 minutes in the freezer until it is set, or bake for 10 minutes in a 350-degree oven. Cool before filling.

VARIATIONS:

The easiest way to vary the recipe is to change the type of crumbs used. Let your imagination soar: graham crackers are standard, but also consider the following possibilities: digestive biscuits, vanilla wafers, ginger snaps, zweiback, matzo, pumpernickle bread, melba toast, stale angel food cake, or leftover spice cake.

Low-calorie Crumb Crust: Although this recipe calls for butter, margarine can be substituted if cholesterol is a worry. If you are concerned about calories, consider the following combination for a low-calorie crust.

3 TABLESPOONS DIET MARGARINE, SOFTENED
¾ CUP GRAHAM CRACKER CRUMBS

In general, use as little margarine as you can and still be able to get the crumbs to press together easily.

Flavored Crumb Crust: Some additional flavorings will enhance your crust further. We suggest adding the following, especially if you are using a bland cracker for your crumbs.

1 TEASPOON GROUND CINNAMON
1 TEASPOON GRATED NUTMEG
1 TEASPOON GRATED LEMON RIND

Add the seasonings after you have blended the butter and sugar with the crumbs, then press the mixture into the baking pan as directed.

Crumb-nut Crust: If you want a little variety in texture, add chopped nuts to the crumb mixture, subtracting the equivalent quantity of crumbs from the final measurements.

Chocolate Crumb Crust: Add 2 tablespoons of unsweetened cocoa to your crumb mixture.

Mocha Crumb Crust: Another way to achieve a different result is to try the following recipe for a coffee and chocolate taste treat.

2 CUPS VANILLA COOKIE CRUMBS
3 TABLESPOONS UNSWEETENED COCOA
1 TEASPOON INSTANT COFFEE POWDER
4 TABLESPOONS BUTTER, MELTED

Mix the ingredients thoroughly, then press the crumbs into the baking pan. Chill until the crumbs are set.

Nut Crust

Whereas in the Basic Crumb Crust you combine cracker crumbs with butter and sugar, in the Nut Crust you blend nuts for a different and equally delicious effect. Again, your choice of nuts is quite open, although we find that walnuts, blanched almonds, or brazil nuts work very well.

This crust is prebaked to bring out the flavor of the nuts. It is recommended for the Walnut Cream Cheesecake and the Basic Cheese Pie.

1 Preheat the oven to 400 degrees.

2 Place all the ingredients in a mixing bowl and blend thoroughly.

3 Press the mixture into the bottom and partly up the sides of a greased 9-inch baking pan or springform mold.

4 Bake for about 6 minutes, or until the crust is a light golden brown. Cool before filling.

YIELDS:
ONE 9-INCH CRUST

INGREDIENTS:
1½ CUPS FINELY CHOPPED NUTS
2 TABLESPOONS GRANULATED
    SUGAR
2 TABLESPOONS BUTTER,
    SOFTENED

Shortbread Crust

YIELDS:
ONE 9-INCH CRUST

This crust is very similar to the famous Scottish shortbread. The flavor of butter predominates and although margarine can be substituted, we don't recommend it. Use it for making The Heavy One, Custard Cheesecake, Pumpkin Cheesecake, the Belgian Cheese Tart, and the French Cheesecake, among others.

The crust can be either prebaked or just chilled. However, for any cake that is baked at a low oven temperature (or that has a particularly liquid filling), it is best to prebake. At temperatures below 350 degrees the crust won't cook thoroughly. Just prebake the bottom crust; don't attempt to prebake the sides because they don't really need the extra baking time and they will collapse anyway.

INGREDIENTS:
1½ CUPS SIFTED ALL-PURPOSE
  FLOUR
¼ TO ⅓ CUP GRANULATED
  SUGAR (TO TASTE)
1 LARGE EGG, SEPARATED, AND
  YOLK LIGHTLY BEATEN
½ CUP BUTTER, SOFTENED

1 If you are prebaking the bottom crust, preheat the oven to 400 degrees.

2 Working on a large flat surface, such as a pastry board, place the flour and sugar in the center and mix together. Form a small depression or well in the center of the mound.

3 Add the beaten yolk and the softened butter to the well, then blend these with the dry mixture. Mix the ingredients thoroughly, using your hands — there's no substitute for warm hands.

4 Shape the dough into a ball and wrap in plastic wrap. Chill for at least 10 minutes.

5 Roll out the dough to a thickness of about ¼ inch. You should have a circle of about 11 inches in diameter. For best results, roll out your dough between 2 sheets of waxed paper, then peel away the paper and cut the crust in a 9-inch circle. Place the circle inside a 9-inch springform mold.

6 If you are prebaking the crust, then prick the crust several times with a fork to keep the crust from puffing up during baking. Place the springform in the oven and bake for 15 to 20 minutes, or until light brown. Allow to cool.

7 Use the leftover dough to form the sides. Press the dough against the sides of the form, smoothing it so as to have a continuous side. Make sure also that the sides meet the bottom crust all the way around. Brush the reserved egg white onto the shell, covering both bottom and sides. This will seal the dough and keep it from becoming soggy.

WORDS TO THE WISE:

One way to save time with this recipe is to skip the first chilling step and proceed right to filling the form with the dough. Press the dough into the pan with your fingers; while the crust won't be as uniformly smooth, that is not particularly noticeable in the finished product.

VARIATIONS:

Flavored Shortbread Crust: For additional flavor, or if you decide to use margarine instead of butter, include the following for some added interest.

1 TEASPOON VANILLA EXTRACT

OR

1 TEASPOON GRATED LEMON RIND

Liqueur-flavored Shortbread Crust: A little bit of liqueur (1 teaspoon) added to the basic Shortbread Crust ingredients along with the egg yolk and butter will give the cheesecake an extra lift.

Spongecake Layer

YIELDS:
ONE 9-INCH LAYER

Essentially this is a thin single cake layer, serving as a bottom crust for some cheesecakes. It is used for the Brandy Cheesecake.

Of necessity, this crust must be prebaked and is best made a day ahead.

INGREDIENTS:
½ TEASPOON BUTTER
1 TABLESPOON HOT WATER
1 LARGE EGG, SEPARATED
¼ CUP SELF-RISING FLOUR
¼ TEASPOON SALT
2 TABLESPOONS
  CONFECTIONERS' SUGAR

1 Preheat the oven to 350 degrees; grease a 9-inch baking pan.

2 Melt the butter in the water. When melted, pour into a medium-sized mixing bowl.

3 Add the egg yolk to the bowl and beat, blending it well with the butter and water.

4 Stir in the flour and salt, making sure there are no lumps.

5 In another bowl, beat the egg white until it forms soft peaks. Then gradually add the sugar, continuing to beat until white is stiff and glossy.

6 Fold the egg white into the flour mixture. Pour into a 9-inch springform pan and smooth surface to an even thickness.

7 Bake for about 12 minutes, or until the cake is firm. Cool.

VARIATIONS:

Flavored Spongecake Layer: For a slightly different taste, add 1 teaspoon of your favorite extract or a teaspoon of rum to the batter.

Spicy Spongecake Layer: Include either or both of the following for a spicy cake layer:

½ TEASPOON GROUND CINNAMON
¼ TEASPOON GRATED NUTMEG OR GROUND CLOVES

Chocolate Spongecake Layer: For a different effect, make your cake layer chocolate-flavored: Add ½ square (½ ounce) melted unsweetened chocolate to your batter.

Basic Pastry Pie Crust

YIELDS:
ONE 9-INCH PIE SHELL

This is the familiar pie crust, also used for endless fruit pies and tarts. If you don't already have your favorite recipe for this, try the following one. It is a good crust for the Buttermilk Cottage Cheese Pie, the Lemon Meringue Cheese Pie, or the English Cheesecake.

The secret to a good pie pastry is to not overhandle the ingredients. Mixing the ingredients too long will make the pastry tough. And when mixing the butter and shortening into the flour, it is best to use chilled ingredients (and utensils, if necessary). Do not mix the ingredients with your hands; use a pastry blender, a knife, or a fork. When adding the water, add just enough to make the flour mixture stick together. Too little water will make the pastry crumbly, and too much will toughen it.

This dough must be prebaked before filling.

INGREDIENTS:
2 CUPS SIFTED ALL-PURPOSE FLOUR
½ TEASPOON SALT
2 TEASPOONS GRANULATED SUGAR
4 TABLESPOONS BUTTER, CHILLED
3 TABLESPOONS SHORTENING, CHILLED
5 TABLESPOONS COLD WATER

1 Sift together the flour, salt, and sugar into a medium-sized mixing bowl.

2 Add the butter to the flour all at once. Mix together until thoroughly blended. Then add the shortening and continue to blend by cutting it into the flour. The mixture will begin to look like crumbs or small pebbles. It will have the texture of oatmeal.

3 Sprinkle the water over the dough, distributing it evenly throughout. The dough will become sticky and cling together. Gather it into a ball and wrap it in plastic wrap. Chill for at least 30 minutes.

4 Preheat the oven to 450 degrees.

5 When the pastry has chilled, roll it out on a pastry board to a thickness of ⅛ inch. The easiest way is to roll the dough between 2 sheets of waxed paper.

6 Roll the dough up onto the rolling pin and transfer it to a 9-inch pie pan. Gently press the pastry down into the pan and up onto the sides. Use the excess pastry around the edges to form flutes, or cut away the excess with a scissors.

7 Prick the bottom of the pastry shell thoroughly to prevent trapped air from bubbling the dough. Butter a sheet of aluminum foil and place the foil down into the shell. Weight it down with weights or beans to keep the crust from lifting up.

8 Bake the crust for 7 to 10 minutes, then remove the weights and the foil. Return the crust to the oven and continue baking for another 8 to 10 minutes, or until the crust is lightly browned.

WORDS TO THE WISE:

If you have difficulty rolling out the dough, do not reroll it; just patch the tears or holes. Rerolling will make the pastry tough.

Whole-Wheat Pie Crust

YIELDS:
ONE 9-INCH PIE SHELL

We're seeing more and more uses of whole-wheat flour in cooking today, including whole-wheat pasta, pizza, and pastries. Here's a recipe for a whole-wheat pie shell, recommended for use with the Tofu Pie.

This dough must be prebaked before filling.

INGREDIENTS:
1 CUP WHOLE-WHEAT FLOUR
3 TABLESPOONS BROWN SUGAR
6 TO 8 TABLESPOONS BUTTER,
   CHILLED
COLD WATER, AS NEEDED

1 Preheat the oven to 350 degrees.

2 Cut the butter into very small pieces.

3 In a large mixing bowl, combine the flour, sugar, and butter. Mix with your fingers until the pastry resembles coarse meal. If necessary, moisten lightly with a few drops of water to make the mixture more workable.

4 Press the mixture into a pie pan, smoothing out the dough to a uniform thickness. Bake the crust for 5 minutes, then allow to cool before filling.

Meringue Pie Shell

YIELDS:
ONE 9-INCH PIE SHELL

This is an interesting variation on the usual cheesecake crust. Try it for an unusual switch in texture and taste with any of the no-bake cheese pies.

When beating the whites, be certain that your beater and bowl are clean and dry. A tiny bit of fat or oil will ruin the meringue. Also be careful when separating the eggs. The yolk must be removed intact so that no bit of it gets into the whites, since that would keep the whites from whipping easily.

High humidity is the enemy of meringues. It will make your meringue weep and go limp. It is best to make this pie shell just before you plan to use it.

1 Preheat the oven to 275 degrees. Butter a 9-inch pie pan liberally, being sure to cover both bottom and sides.

2 In a large mixing bowl, beat the egg whites, cream of tartar, and salt until frothy.

3 Gradually add the sugar, continuing to beat until whites are stiff and glossy.

4 Quickly stir in the nuts, then pour the mixture into a 9-inch pie pan, smoothing it to conform to the shape of the pan.

5 Bake the meringue for 1 to 1½ hours, or until light brown and crisp throughout. Cool to room temperature, then fill.

INGREDIENTS:
3 EGG WHITES, AT ROOM
    TEMPERATURE
¼ TEASPOON CREAM OF TARTAR
⅛ TEASPOON SALT
½ CUP CONFECTIONERS' SUGAR
¼ CUP FINELY CHOPPED NUTS

VARIATION:

For a truly spectacular dessert, make some additional meringue for decoration. Fill a pastry tube with the meringue and pipe it along the edge of the pan.

Torte Crust

We recommend this quick and simple pastry crust for the Apple Bavarian Torte, but it should also work quite well with any of the recipes where a pastry crust is called for. It is easy to make by hand, and even easier to prepare with a food processor.

This crust must be prebaked before filling.

INGREDIENTS:
½ CUP BUTTER, CHILLED
1 CUP SIFTED ALL-PURPOSE
   FLOUR
⅓ CUP GRANULATED SUGAR
¼ TEASPOON VANILLA EXTRACT

1 Preheat the oven to 350 degrees.

2 Cut the butter into very small pieces.

3 In a large bowl, combine the flour, sugar, butter pieces, and vanilla. Mix together with your fingers until the pastry resembles coarse meal.

4 Press the dough into a pie pan and bake for 5 minutes.

Charlotte Crust

YIELDS:
ONE CRUST, OF VARYING SHAPE

The charlotte is a traditional French dessert in which a round mold is lined with sponge fingers, then filled with Bavarian cream, fruit, or pastry cream. The English use small sponge cakes for trifle, a dessert of layers of sherry-soaked cake, custard, fruits or ham, and whipped cream. You also can use little sponge cakes, or ladyfingers, to serve as the crust for some of your cheesecakes. We've noted one use in this book — the Trifling Cheesecake —

but try some others of your own devising. Be sure, however, that the filling you choose is a somewhat stiff one. If you use a very liquid filling, the ladyfingers will quickly become soggy.

INGREDIENTS:
1 DOZEN PLAIN LADYFINGERS

1 Split the ladyfingers in half lengthwise if they are not already split commercially.

2 Arrange them to line your baking dish or mold, both bottom and sides. Cut the tops of any that extend beyond the rim of the mold. Try making decorative patterns.

3 Fill immediately with desired filling and bake.

VARIATION:

Trifle Crust: This recipe is for the Trifling Cheesecake.

1 DOZEN LADYFINGERS
⅓ CUP MEDIUM OR CREAM SHERRY
2 TABLESPOONS WATER
¼ CUP STRAWBERRY JAM

1 Split the ladyfingers in half lengthwise if they have not been split already.

2 Arrange the ladyfingers to line the bottom and sides of a 2-quart rectangular baking dish. Trim off the excess bits of cake so that the lining is smooth throughout. Patch where necessary.

3 Mix together the sherry and water, then sprinkle the mixture over the ladyfingers. You want to flavor them to the point of being damp, not soggy.

4 Dot the ladyfinger lining of the pan with bits of the jam.

Muerbeteig (or Mürbeteig)

This is a sweet-dough crust used for the German Käsekuchen. Note the baking powder included in the ingredients; it makes the dough rise slightly while the cake bakes. Be sure to use only a thin layer of dough to line the pan.

INGREDIENTS:
2 CUPS SIFTED ALL-PURPOSE
  FLOUR
4 TABLESPOONS BUTTER
½ CUP GRANULATED SUGAR
1 LARGE EGG
1 TEASPOON BAKING POWDER

1 In a large mixing bowl, blend all the ingredients, cutting in the butter and working the mixture with your hands until it is thoroughly mixed and workable.

2 Divide the dough into 2 equal portions. Use one half to line the bottom of a greased 9-inch springform pan, the other to line the sides. Either roll out the dough or press mixture into pan with your fingers. Chill before filling.

VARIATIONS:

Hungarian Crust: The crust for the Hungarian Cheesecake is very similar, but could also be used with many other fillings.

1½ CUPS SIFTED ALL-PURPOSE FLOUR
1 TEASPOON BAKING POWDER
4 TABLESPOONS BUTTER
2 EGG YOLKS, LIGHTLY BEATEN
⅛ TEASPOON SALT
1 TABLESPOON LEMON JUICE
3 TO 4 TABLESPOONS COLD WATER

1 Sift together the flour and baking powder, then set aside.

2 Cream the butter in a large mixing bowl, then add the yolks, salt, and lemon juice. Mix well.

3 Add the dry mixture, then, using your fingers, work the dough to a smooth consistency. Add the water as necessary to work the dough.

4 Roll the dough out on a flat surface to a thickness of ¼ inch. Cut the dough to fit your greased pan and place it in. Use the excess to fit around the sides of the pan. Chill.

WORDS TO THE WISE:

If you prefer, or if you are having trouble rolling out the dough, simply press it into the form, shaping it to match the contours of the mold.

Old World Crust: This crust is used for the Old World Cheesecake. It is a simpler, plainer crust than those previously described.

1¼ CUPS SIFTED ALL-PURPOSE FLOUR
¾ TEASPOON BAKING POWDER
¼ TEASPOON SALT
¼ CUP BUTTER

1 In a large mixing bowl, combine the ingredients and mix well, working in the butter with your hands.

2 Shape the dough into a greased 13 × 9 × 2-inch baking dish, pressing it against the bottom and sides and into the corners. Chill well before filling.

Sweet Yeast Crust

YIELDS:
ONE 9-INCH CRUST

INGREDIENTS:
1 TABLESPOON (1 PACKAGE)
   ACTIVE DRY YEAST
¼ CUP WARM WATER
2 CUPS SIFTED ALL-PURPOSE
   FLOUR
¼ CUP GRANULATED SUGAR
½ TEASPOON SALT
½ CUP MILK
¼ CUP BUTTER
1 LARGE EGG, LIGHTLY BEATEN

This lightly sweetened yeast dough is the recommended accompaniment for the Czechoslovakian and Polish Cheesecakes. Beginners may find it a bit of a challenge, but if you have ever baked your own bread, this recipe should prove quite easy. Keep in mind that the liquid ingredients must be lukewarm, not hot.

1 Lightly grease the baking pan.

2 Dissolve the yeast in the water.

3 In a large mixing bowl, mix together the flour, sugar, and salt.

4 In a saucepan, heat the milk and butter, then cool to lukewarm. Add the warm milk and the yeast mixture to the dry ingredients, then add the egg. Mix thoroughly to form a moist, soft dough. Knead lightly until the dough is soft and smooth.

5 Cover the dough with a towel and set the bowl to rise in a warm place. The dough should rise to twice its original size, approximately 1 hour.

6 When the dough has doubled in bulk, punch it down and pat it into a thin layer. Place the layer into the bottom of the pan. Use remaining dough to line the sides of the pan. (It is difficult, and unnecessary, to line the sides of the pan all the way to the top; as the crust bakes, it will rise to near the top anyway.)

7 Allow the dough to rise again in the pan until again doubled in bulk, about 30 to 45 minutes.

8 When dough has doubled again, crust is ready to be filled.

The Simplest Crust of All

By far the easiest, and sometimes the most appropriate, crust is a simple dusting to coat the bottom and sides of the baking dish. Again, your choices are almost limitless. We suggest using fruit, nuts, or a crumb mixture, but you may have your own ideas.

1 Butter the baking dish, pie pan, or springform mold until generously coated.

2 Sprinkle crumbs as needed into the pan, then turn the pan around and shake gently, distributing the crumbs along the sides as well. The crumbs should completely coat the inside of the pan.

3 Chill briefly to set the crumbs, then fill with desired filling.

VARIATIONS:

Simple Nut Crust: Instead of using crumbs, as directed above, substitute finely chopped nuts such as walnuts.

Simple Fruit Crust: Instead of using crumbs or nuts, substitute fresh fruit pieces or small fruit such as blueberries.

YIELDS:
ONE CRUST, OF VARYING SHAPE

INGREDIENTS:
1 TO 2 TABLESPOONS BUTTER
½ TO ⅔ CUP FINE BREAD
    CRUMBS

Toppings and Glazes

$\mathcal{F}$rankly, we think that nine times out of ten you just can't top the taste of a creamy white cheesecake all by itself. Putting a topping on many cheesecakes is just gilding the lily; usually we prefer to garnish the cakes with fresh fruit. Sometimes, though, we've found that the right topping can bring a whole new dimension to a familiar cheesecake. We list here some of our favorite toppings, and each recipe yields enough for one cake. Which ones go best with your favorite cheesecakes we leave to you to decide.

Whipped Cream Topping

What could be easier than whipping up some cream? Only eating it.

INGREDIENTS:
1 CUP HEAVY CREAM
3 TABLESPOONS
    CONFECTIONERS' SUGAR
1 EGG WHITE

1 In a chilled bowl, beat the cream, confectioners' sugar, and egg white until the mixture is stiff.

2 Spread the topping on the cake shortly before serving.

VARIATION:

For an interesting change, try folding in any of the following:

½ TEASPOON VANILLA EXTRACT
⅓ CUP CHOPPED NUTS
⅓ CUP GRATED COCONUT
⅓ CUP JAM
½ CUP FINELY CHOPPED FRUIT
½ CUP BROWN SUGAR
⅓ CUP CRUSHED HARD CANDY

Sour-Cream Topping

Sour cream provides a piquant contrast to a sweet cheesecake and can hide a blemish or two from even the most prying of eyes.

INGREDIENTS:
1 CUP SOUR CREAM
2 TABLESPOONS GRANULATED
    SUGAR
1 TEASPOON VANILLA EXTRACT

1 Preheat the oven to 450 degrees, if not already hot from baking the cake.

2 In a bowl, gently stir together the sour cream, sugar, and vanilla.

3 Spread the mixture over the top of a warm cake and bake for 5 to 7 minutes, or until set.

Meringue Topping

A meringue can turn any pasty white cheesecake into a golden beauty. Don't forget to include the ten minutes necessary for the meringue in the total baking time for the cake.

1 Preheat the oven to 350 degrees.

2 In a large mixing bowl, beat the egg whites, cream of tartar, and salt until the whites are frothy.

3 Gradually add the sugar, beating until the whites are stiff and glossy.

4 Spread the mixture over the cake, or use a pastry bag and nozzle to make a decorated top. Bake the cake until the topping has set, about 10 minutes.

INGREDIENTS:
4 EGG WHITES, AT ROOM
    TEMPERATURE
¼ TEASPOON CREAM OF TARTAR
⅛ TEASPOON SALT
½ CUP SIFTED CONFECTIONERS'
    SUGAR

Honey Glaze

If you think we scrimp on the sugar in the cheesecakes, this is the topping for you. It's solid sweet.

INGREDIENTS:
2 TABLESPOONS
   CONFECTIONERS' SUGAR
⅓ CUP HONEY
1 TABLESPOON BUTTER

1 Combine all the ingredients in a small saucepan and bring to a boil over medium heat, stirring frequently. Remove from the heat.

2 Cool the mixture to just over room temperature, then spread it on the cake. Chill before serving.

Chocolate Glaze

This is a very rich chocolate glaze sure to satisfy even the most avid chocolate lover.

INGREDIENTS:
6 SQUARES (6 OUNCES)
   SEMISWEET CHOCOLATE
¼ CUP BUTTER
¾ CUP CONFECTIONERS' SUGAR
1 TEASPOON VANILLA EXTRACT
¼ CUP WATER

1 Melt the chocolate and butter in the top of a double boiler. Remove from the heat.

2 Stir in the sugar, vanilla, and water and blend well.

3 Spread the mixture over the cake, then chill before serving.

Apricot Glaze

This is a generous recipe. If you prefer apricots in smaller doses, cut the quantities in half. Other dried fruits may be substituted, or mix up your own wild combination.

1 Boil the apricots in the water until they are very soft. Pour the fruit through a strainer, pressing the fruit through, or simply drain excess water and beat at high speed until smooth.

2 Stir together the strained fruit with the sugar and the syrup. Cook over medium heat until the sugar is dissolved. Remove from the heat.

3 Cool to room temperature, then spread the mixture over the cooled cheesecake. Chill before serving.

INGREDIENTS:
2 CUPS (11 OUNCES) DRIED
  APRICOTS
1 CUP WATER
½ CUP GRANULATED SUGAR
1 CUP LIGHT CORN SYRUP

Cranberry Topping

The tart flavor of cranberries and their striking color make this an exciting addition to any cheesecake.

INGREDIENTS:
1 CUP GRANULATED SUGAR
1 CUP WATER
1 TEASPOON GRATED ORANGE
　RIND
¼ TEASPOON GROUND CLOVES
2 CUPS FRESH CRANBERRIES

1 In a medium saucepan, stir together the sugar, water, orange rind, cloves, and cranberries. Cook over medium heat, stirring to dissolve the sugar.

2 When the berries begin to pop open, remove the saucepan from the heat and cool to room temperature. Pour off the excess liquid.

3 Spoon the mixture over the cheesecake, then chill until set, about 4 hours.

Lemon Glaze

Lemon is commonly used as flavoring in cheesecake fillings. It's also good on top. Substitute lime or even grapefruit if you like.

INGREDIENTS:
1 TABLESPOON BUTTER
⅓ CUP GRANULATED SUGAR
1 LARGE EGG
1 TABLESPOON LEMON JUICE

1 Melt the butter in the top of a double boiler. Stir in the sugar, egg, and lemon juice quickly, then cook until the mixture is thick, about 10 minutes.

2 Cool, then spread the glaze over a cooled cake. Chill before serving.

Walnut Cream-Cheese Cake

Dark Sweet Cherry Topping

Much better than anything you could spoon out of a can labeled "pie filling," this topping is also not at all difficult to make. Add more sugar if you like your cherries extra sweet.

1 Drain the cherries and save ½ cup of the syrup.

2 Combine the sugar and cornstarch in a small saucepan. Slowly add the syrup, water, and lemon juice, heating the mixture over medium heat. Stir constantly until the sugar dissolves and the liquid comes to a rapid boil.

3 Stir the mixture for about 3 minutes more, or until the mixture thickens and clears. Remove from the heat, then stir in the brandy and the butter. Cool to room temperature.

4 Arrange the cherries on the cake. Pour the cooled mixture over the cherries. Refrigerate until set, about 4 hours.

INGREDIENTS:

1 JAR (17 OUNCES) PITTED, DARK, SWEET CHERRIES IN HEAVY SYRUP
1 TABLESPOON GRANULATED SUGAR
1 TABLESPOON CORNSTARCH
¼ CUP WATER
1 TEASPOON LEMON JUICE
1 TEASPOON BRANDY
1 TEASPOON BUTTER

Pineapple Topping

If you're feeling artistic, substitute pineapple rings for crushed pineapple and create a design on the cake, then pour the glaze over it to set.

INGREDIENTS:
⅓ CUP GRANULATED SUGAR
2 TABLESPOONS CORNSTARCH
1 CAN (20 OUNCES)
  UNSWEETENED CRUSHED
  PINEAPPLE
1 TABLESPOON LEMON JUICE
1 TEASPOON BUTTER

1 Stir together the sugar and cornstarch in a medium saucepan.

2 Drain the pineapple, then add the juice to the sugar and cornstarch. Stir in the lemon juice and blend well.

3 Cook over medium heat, stirring constantly, until the mixture boils. Boil for 2 minutes, or until thick and clear.

4 Add the pineapple and butter, and remove from the heat. Cool to room temperature, then spread onto a cooled cheesecake.

Strawberry Glaze

Fresh fruit may travel better if it's fixed to the cake with a glaze, and a touch of lemon juice can bring out the flavor in many fruits. Frozen fruit may also be used. Experiment.

1. Hull and wash the berries. Crush enough berries to make a cup of pulp. Cut the remaining ones in half and arrange them on the cake.

2. In a small saucepan, mix together the sugar and the cornstarch. Add the water and stir to dissolve.

3. Add the berry pulp to the saucepan and bring to a rapid boil. Stir constantly while the mixture boils for 2 minutes.

4. Remove the saucepan from the heat and add the butter and lemon juice. Let the mixture cool to room temperature, then pour the glaze over the strawberries. Refrigerate until set, about 4 hours.

INGREDIENTS:
1 QUART FRESH STRAWBERRIES,
    OR OTHER FRESH BERRIES
½ CUP GRANULATED SUGAR
2 TABLESPOONS CORNSTARCH
¼ CUP WATER
1 TEASPOON BUTTER
1 TEASPOON LEMON JUICE

Cream-Cheese Cakes

$\mathcal{C}$ream-cheese cheesecakes are the American contribution to an art that probably began when the first shepherd discovered curd. With the advent of cream cheese, cheesecakes became smoother, richer, more luscious than ever before, truly the most opulent of desserts.

Heavy Cheesecake

RECOMMENDATIONS:
BASIC CRUMB CRUST (PAGE 46),
    MADE FROM DIGESTIVE
    BISCUITS
9-INCH SPRINGFORM PAN

INGREDIENTS:
1 POUND CREAM CHEESE
1 CUP GRANULATED SUGAR
3 LARGE EGGS
1 TEASPOON GRATED LEMON
    RIND
1 TABLESPOON LEMON JUICE
½ CUP SELF-RISING FLOUR
1 CUP SOUR CREAM

When you think cheesecake, this is probably the one that comes to mind — a heavy cake, not too sweet and not too dry. Take care not to leave this one in the oven too long, as it will dry out and harden.

1 Preheat the oven to 325 degrees.

2 In a large mixing bowl, beat together the cream cheese, sugar, and eggs until smooth and light.

3 Add the lemon rind, lemon juice, and flour and mix into the cheese mixture.

4 Stir in the sour cream, just enough to blend together.

5 Pour the mixture into the prepared crust and bake for 45 minutes. Allow to cool in the oven for 30 additional minutes.

6 Prop the oven door open and allow the cake to cool further — to room temperature. Chill.

7 Serve the cake chilled, with whipped cream and sprinkled with cinnamon.

Heavy Layered Cheesecake

This one may remind you of that favorite dairy-case brand, but once you taste it, you'll find that there is really no comparison. This is an ideal cheesecake for beginners; not only is it very simple to make, but if you do wind up with minor flaws or blemishes, the top layer of sour cream will hide them for you. Be sure, though, to spread the sour-cream topping smoothly; it won't settle in the oven.

1 Preheat the oven to 350 degrees.

2 In a large mixing bowl, beat together the cream cheese and sugar until light and fluffy.

3 Add the eggs, one at a time, beating thoroughly after each.

4 Add the lemon rind and vanilla, then mix briefly.

5 Pour the mixture into the prepared crust and bake for about 55 minutes, or until center is firm to the touch. Remove the cake from the oven. Adjust the oven temperature to 450 degrees.

6 Prepare the sour-cream topping by gently stirring together the sour cream, sugar, and vanilla. Spread this mixture over the top of the cake.

7 Place the cake back in the oven and bake for 8 to 10 additional minutes, or until the topping has set. Remove the cake from the oven and cool to room temperature. Chill until ready to serve.

RECOMMENDATIONS:
BASIC CRUMB CRUST (PAGE 46),
    MADE FROM VANILLA WAFERS
9-INCH SPRINGFORM PAN
SOUR-CREAM TOPPING, AS GIVEN
    IN RECIPE

INGREDIENTS:
1 POUND CREAM CHEESE
¾ CUP GRANULATED SUGAR
3 LARGE EGGS
½ TEASPOON GRATED LEMON
    RIND
1 TEASPOON VANILLA EXTRACT

SOUR-CREAM TOPPING:
1 CUP SOUR CREAM
2 TABLESPOONS GRANULATED
    SUGAR
1 TEASPOON VANILLA EXTRACT

New York Cheesecake

RECOMMENDATIONS:
BASIC CRUMB CRUST (PAGE 46),
   MADE FROM MATZO
9-INCH SPRINGFORM PAN

INGREDIENTS:
2 POUNDS CREAM CHEESE
¾ CUP GRANULATED SUGAR
2 LARGE EGGS, LIGHTLY BEATEN
1 TEASPOON VANILLA EXTRACT
2 TABLESPOONS CORNSTARCH
1 CUP SOUR CREAM

This is it; the genuine article. Although simple to make, this classic cheesecake has a complex character. It stands tall, with a slightly cakelike texture.

1 Preheat the oven to 400 degrees.

2 In a large mixing bowl, beat together the cream cheese and sugar until smooth and light.

3 Beat in the eggs, vanilla, and cornstarch, only until thoroughly mixed.

4 Stir in the sour cream until the mixture is well blended.

5 Pour the mixture into the prepared crust and bake for 45 minutes. Allow the cake to cool in the oven, with the door propped slightly open, for 3 hours. Chill.

The Heavy One

This is the richest of cheesecakes and naturally it is the most expensive to make. Well worth every penny, this ten-inch New York-style cheesecake can easily satisfy sixteen people.

1 Preheat the oven to 475 degrees.

2 In a large mixing bowl, beat the cream cheese until it is light and fluffy.

3 Mix in the sugar and flour, and continue beating until smooth.

4 Add the grated rinds, then the yolks and whole eggs, one at a time, beating after each until the mixture is thoroughly blended.

5 Stir in the heavy cream and mix only briefly.

6 Pour the mixture into the prepared crust and bake for 15 minutes at 475 degrees, then reduce the oven temperature to 200 degrees and continue to bake for another hour.

7 When the cake is done, turn off the oven and allow the cake to cool slowly for an additional hour. Remove the cake from the oven and cool to room temperature. Chill before serving.

RECOMMENDATIONS:
SHORTBREAD CRUST (PAGE 50)
10-INCH SPRINGFORM PAN

INGREDIENTS:
2½ POUNDS CREAM CHEESE
1¾ CUPS GRANULATED SUGAR
3 TABLESPOONS ALL-PURPOSE FLOUR
½ TEASPOON GRATED LEMON RIND
½ TEASPOON GRATED ORANGE RIND
2 EGG YOLKS
5 LARGE EGGS
¼ CUP HEAVY CREAM

Barebottom Cheesecake

RECOMMENDATIONS:
BASIC CRUMB CRUST (PAGE 46)
9-INCH SPRINGFORM PAN

INGREDIENTS:
1½ POUNDS CREAM CHEESE
1 CUP GRANULATED SUGAR
2 TABLESPOONS ALL-PURPOSE
    FLOUR
6 LARGE EGGS, SEPARATED
2 TEASPOONS LEMON JUICE
1 TEASPOON VANILLA EXTRACT
1 CUP SOUR CREAM

We call this one the Barebottom Cheesecake because it works well even without a crust — great if you are in a hurry or if you don't have any crumbs on hand. This is one of the cheesecakes we tested on the customers of the Sheepshead Café in Iowa City. It proved to be one of the most popular ones ever served there. It tends to crack easily, but no matter.

1 Preheat the oven to 325 degrees.

2 In a large mixing bowl, beat the cream cheese, sugar, and flour until light and fluffy, about 5 minutes.

3 Add the egg yolks, one at a time, beating thoroughly after each until the mixture is smooth and blended.

4 Add the lemon juice and the vanilla, then also stir in the sour cream.

5 Whip the egg whites until they form soft peaks, then fold into the cream-cheese mixture.

6 Pour the mixture into the prepared crust or into an ungreased baking pan and bake for 1 hour, 10 minutes, until the center of the cake is firm.

7 Cool the cake in the oven for 1 hour, with the door cracked open, then cool to room temperature. Chill.

Connie's Cheesecake

A very light and moist cake, this one will melt in your mouth. It will rise quite high in the oven, and then fall slightly, so no peeking until after the first hour because a draft could ruin it. Be sure to use a pan with a tall (three-inch) collar.

1 Preheat the oven to 325 degrees.

2 In a large mixing bowl, beat the cream cheese with the sugar until fluffy, about 5 minutes.

3 Add the flour and vanilla and continue beating.

4 Mix in the egg yolks, one at a time, beating thoroughly after each.

5 Add the light cream and mix thoroughly.

6 Whip the egg whites until they are stiff, then fold them into the cream-cheese mixture.

7 Pour the mixture into the prepared crust, and bake for 1 hour, 15 minutes, or until the center is firm. Cool to room temperature on a rack, then chill.

RECOMMENDATIONS:
BASIC CRUMB CRUST (PAGE 46)
9-INCH SPRINGFORM PAN

INGREDIENTS:
1 POUND CREAM CHEESE
½ CUP GRANULATED SUGAR
2 TABLESPOONS ALL-PURPOSE
  FLOUR
1 TEASPOON VANILLA EXTRACT
4 LARGE EGGS, SEPARATED
1 CUP LIGHT CREAM, OR ½ CUP
  HEAVY CREAM AND ½ CUP
  MILK

Angel Cheesecake

RECOMMENDATIONS:
BASIC CRUMB CRUST (PAGE 46)
9-INCH SPRINGFORM PAN

INGREDIENTS:
1 POUND CREAM CHEESE
1 TEASPOON GRATED LEMON RIND
2 TEASPOONS LEMON JUICE
1 TEASPOON VANILLA EXTRACT
5 LARGE EGGS, SEPARATED
2 CUPS SOUR CREAM
½ CUP GRANULATED SUGAR

This heavenly cheesecake is the lightest in our collection. Expect it to rise high in the oven and then fall back a bit on cooling. To avoid cracking, be careful not to overbeat or overheat, and allow the cake to cool slowly.

1 Preheat the oven to 325 degrees.

2 In a large mixing bowl, beat the cream cheese until it is light and then add the lemon rind, lemon juice, and vanilla. Mix to blend.

3 Beat in the egg yolks, one at a time, thoroughly mixing after each one, then gently stir in the sour cream.

4 Beat the egg whites until they form soft peaks, then slowly add the sugar, continuing to beat until the whites form stiff peaks.

5 Fold the egg whites into the cream-cheese mixture.

6 Pour the mixture into the prepared crust and bake for 1 hour, 15 minutes. Cool for 10 minutes in the oven with the door open, then run a knife around the edge of the cake to separate it from the pan. Cool at room temperature. Chill.

Kilimanjaro Cheesecake

This is a very striking ivory-white cheesecake. As always, handle the egg whites with care.

1 Preheat the oven to 350 degrees.

2 In a large mixing bowl, beat the cream cheese with the vanilla until soft and fluffy.

3 Beat the egg whites until they form soft peaks, then slowly beat in the sugar until whites form stiff peaks.

4 Fold the egg whites into the cream-cheese mixture.

5 Pour the mixture into the prepared crust and bake for 25 minutes.

6 Meanwhile, prepare the sour-cream topping. In a mixing bowl, stir together the sour cream and the sugar to blend.

7 After the cake has baked for the allotted time, remove from the oven and turn up the temperature to 450 degrees. Spread the sour-cream topping over the top of the cake.

8 Return the cake to the oven and bake at 450 degrees for about 5 minutes. Cool to room temperature then chill.

RECOMMENDATIONS:
FLAVORED CRUMB CRUST
  (PAGE 47)
9-INCH SPRINGFORM PAN
SOUR-CREAM TOPPING, AS GIVEN
  IN RECIPE

INGREDIENTS:
1½ POUNDS CREAM CHEESE
2 TEASPOONS VANILLA EXTRACT
4 EGG WHITES
1 CUP GRANULATED SUGAR

SOUR-CREAM TOPPING:
2 CUPS SOUR CREAM
3 TABLESPOONS GRANULATED
  SUGAR

Snow-White Cheesecake

INGREDIENTS:
1 POUND CREAM CHEESE
1 TEASPOON VANILLA EXTRACT
1 CUP GRANULATED SUGAR
2 CUPS SOUR CREAM
4 EGG WHITES
1 TEASPOON CONFECTIONERS'
 SUGAR

Seven dwarves could easily be led astray by this ivory-white beauty. If you add a couple of yolks, you will get a creamier cake, but you will lose the snow-white effect. Other possible variations are to substitute *carefully drained* vanilla or coffee yogurt for the sour cream. The result is a distinctive and delicious flavor combination that would be hard to put your finger on.

1 Preheat the oven to 350 degrees.

2 In a large mixing bowl, beat together the cream cheese, vanilla, and sugar.

3 Add the sour cream slowly to the mixture.

4 Beat the egg whites until they form soft peaks, then gradually add the confectioners' sugar and continue beating until they form stiff peaks. Fold the egg whites into the cream-cheese mixture.

5 Pour the mixture into the prepared crust, and bake for about 1 hour. Allow to cool in the oven with the door propped open. Chill.

Lunar Cheesecake

Now we know why the man in the moon is smiling. This light, dry cheesecake is out of this world.

1 Preheat the oven to 275 degrees.

2 In a large mixing bowl, beat the cream cheese with 1⅓ cups sugar and the flour until the mixture is smooth and light.

3 Add the egg yolks, one at a time, thoroughly blending after each.

4 Beat the egg whites until they form soft peaks, then gradually add the remaining sugar; continue beating until the whites form stiff peaks.

5 Stir the sour cream and the vanilla into the cheese mixture. Gently fold the egg whites into the batter.

6 Pour the mixture into the prepared crust and bake for about 1 hour, 30 minutes. Cool in the oven with the door ajar. Chill.

RECOMMENDATIONS:
BASIC CRUMB CRUST (PAGE 46),
     MADE FROM VANILLA WAFERS
9-INCH SPRINGFORM PAN

INGREDIENTS:
1½ POUNDS CREAM CHEESE
1⅔ CUPS CONFECTIONERS'
     SUGAR
1 TABLESPOON ALL-PURPOSE
     FLOUR
7 LARGE EGGS, SEPARATED
2 CUPS SOUR CREAM
2 TEASPOONS VANILLA EXTRACT

Custard Cheesecake

RECOMMENDATIONS:
SHORTBREAD CRUST (PAGE 50)
9-INCH SPRINGFORM PAN
FLAVORED-SUGAR TOPPING, AS
  GIVEN IN RECIPE

INGREDIENTS:
½ POUND CREAM CHEESE
½ CUP GRANULATED SUGAR
1 TABLESPOON ALL-PURPOSE
  FLOUR
4 LARGE EGGS
2 CUPS MILK
½ TEASPOON LEMON JUICE
1 TEASPOON VANILLA EXTRACT

FLAVORED-SUGAR TOPPING:
1 TEASPOON GROUND
  CINNAMON
1 TABLESPOON GRANULATED
  SUGAR

This is the most moist cheesecake in our collection; it is really a custard at heart.

1 Preheat the oven to 350 degrees.

2 In a large mixing bowl, beat the cream cheese with the sugar and flour until the mixture is smooth and fluffy.

3 Add the eggs, one at a time, beating thoroughly after each.

4 Add the milk slowly, continuing to beat slowly. Then add the lemon juice and the vanilla.

5 Pour the mixture into the prepared crust.

6 Mix the cinnamon with the sugar and sprinkle it over the top of the cake.

7 Bake the cake for 55 to 60 minutes, or until a knife comes out clean. Cool to room temperature, then chill.

Walnut Cream-Cheese Cake

This is really a cake with cream cheese in it, rather than a cheesecake, but it is delicious. The flavors and textures of the nuts and cheese complement each other perfectly. Don't serve this one chilled — it is much softer and moister at room temperature.

1 Preheat the oven to 300 degrees.

2 Sift together the flour, baking powder, and salt and set aside.

3 In a large mixing bowl, cream the butter while adding the cream cheese, lemon rind, and sugar. Beat until smooth.

4 Beat in the eggs, one at a time, until incorporated. The batter may appear slightly curdled, but don't worry about it.

5 Gradually add the dry mixture to the batter, then stir in the walnuts.

6 Pour the batter into the prepared pan and bake for about 1 hour, 20 minutes, or until a knife comes out clean. Serve at room temperature.

RECOMMENDATIONS:
SIMPLE NUT CRUST (PAGE 63), WITH WALNUTS
2-QUART BUNDT OR KUGELHOPF PAN

INGREDIENTS:
2 CUPS SIFTED ALL-PURPOSE FLOUR
2 TEASPOONS BAKING POWDER
½ TEASPOON SALT
1 CUP BUTTER
½ POUND CREAM CHEESE
1 TEASPOON GRATED LEMON RIND
1½ CUPS GRANULATED SUGAR
4 LARGE EGGS
¼ CUP MEDIUM-CHOPPED WALNUTS

Specialty Cheesecakes

*S*pecialty cheesecakes are just that — special! Even those with an ingrained revulsion to cream cheese when it is spread raw and naked on a cracker will find temptation irresistible when faced with the full range of this versatile dessert. Whether you prefer sherry, pineapple, chocolate, almond, or pumpkin, there's a cake for you. In fact, the possibilities are really only limited by your imagination. We may have written the book, but we won't have the last word.

Currant Cheesecake

RECOMMENDATIONS:
BASIC CRUMB CRUST (PAGE 46)
9-INCH SPRINGFORM PAN
CONFECTIONERS'-SUGAR
    TOPPING, AS GIVEN IN RECIPE

INGREDIENTS:
½ CUP DRIED CURRANTS
¼ CUP + 5 TABLESPOONS
    ALL-PURPOSE FLOUR
1 POUND CREAM CHEESE
1¼ CUPS GRANULATED SUGAR
5 LARGE EGGS, SEPARATED
2 TEASPOONS LEMON JUICE
1 TEASPOON GRATED LEMON
    RIND
1½ TEASPOONS VANILLA
    EXTRACT
1¼ CUPS SOUR CREAM
⅛ TEASPOON SALT
CONFECTIONERS' SUGAR

You'll be swept away by the currants with your first bite of this delightfully rich cheesecake. Although fairly stiff and straight, it is enlivened by the sharp contrast of flavors. If you can't find currants, substitute chopped raisins.

1 Preheat the oven to 325 degrees.

2 Mix the currants with the ¼ cup flour so that fruits are loose and separated. Add the excess to the remaining flour measure.

3 In a large mixing bowl, beat the cream cheese and sugar until they are light and fluffy.

4 Add the yolks, one at a time, beating thoroughly after each one.

5 Add the remaining flour and the lemon juice, lemon rind, vanilla, and sour cream, beating until the mixture is smooth. Stir in the currants.

6 Beat the egg whites with the salt until they form stiff peaks. Fold the whites into the cream-cheese mixture.

7 Pour the mixture into the prepared crust and bake for 50 minutes, or until the center no longer looks soft. Turn the oven off and leave the cake inside to cool for an additional 40 minutes. Remove the cake from the oven and cool to room temperature.

8 Dust with confectioners' sugar and serve at room temperature.

Ginger Cheesecake

If you like the warm taste of ginger, try this cake. But if you want it even hotter, add a couple of tablespoons of freshly grated gingerroot. The combination may not sound very good, but it tastes and smells just fine.

1 Preheat the oven to 300 degrees.

2 In a large mixing bowl, beat the cream cheese and sugar until smooth and light.

3 Add the eggs, cream, vanilla, and ginger and beat until they are thoroughly mixed with the cream cheese.

4 Pour into the prepared crust and bake for 1 hour, 40 minutes. Turn off the oven but leave the cake in for another hour. Cool on a rack to room temperature, then chill.

RECOMMENDATIONS:
BASIC CRUMB CRUST (PAGE 46),
    MADE FROM GINGER SNAPS
9-INCH SPRINGFORM PAN

INGREDIENTS:
2 POUNDS CREAM CHEESE
1¼ CUPS GRANULATED SUGAR
4 LARGE EGGS, LIGHTLY BEATEN
½ CUP HEAVY CREAM
1 TEASPOON VANILLA EXTRACT
½ CUP FINELY CHOPPED
    CANDIED GINGER

Almond Cheesecake

RECOMMENDATIONS:
CRUMB-NUT CRUST (PAGE 48),
   MADE FROM GRAHAM
   CRACKERS AND ALMONDS
9-INCH SPRINGFORM PAN

INGREDIENTS:
1 POUND CREAM CHEESE
¾ CUP GRANULATED SUGAR
3 LARGE EGGS
1 TEASPOON VANILLA EXTRACT
½ TEASPOON ALMOND EXTRACT
⅓ CUP CHOPPED ALMONDS
3 CUPS SOUR CREAM

This might look like the poor man's version of the Hazelnut Cheesecake (if you haven't priced sour cream lately), but note that replacing a pound of cream cheese with sour cream gives a lighter, softer cheesecake with that tang of sour cream.

1 Preheat the oven to 375 degrees.

2 In a large mixing bowl, beat together the cream cheese and sugar until the mixture is light and fluffy.

3 Add the eggs, one at a time, beating thoroughly after each.

4 Add the extracts, almonds, and sour cream and mix until ingredients are well blended.

5 Pour the mixture into the prepared crust and bake for about 1 hour, or until set. Cool to room temperature, then chill.

Hazelnut Cheesecake

A wonderful, truly excessive cheesecake that must be tasted to be believed. You can vary the quantity of nuts to suit your taste and pocketbook, since even one-third cup of nuts is enough to give the cake a hint of that wonderful flavor. Toasting the nuts is important, however. Untoasted nuts just won't have nearly as much flavor, and they will tend to soften during baking as well.

1 Preheat the oven to 300 degrees.

2 In a large mixing bowl, beat together the cream cheese, sugar, and vanilla until smooth.

3 Add the eggs, beating until the mixture is fluffy.

4 Beat in the heavy cream, then stir in the nuts.

5 Pour the mixture into the prepared crust and bake for 2 hours. Cool the cake in the oven for 1 hour, then cool to room temperature. Serve at room temperature.

WORDS TO THE WISE:

To toast the hazelnuts, preheat the oven to 400 degrees. Place the nuts on a cookie sheet and bake them until they are evenly browned, about 10 minutes. Stir the nuts occasionally as they brown. If the nuts still have their paperlike skins on, sift the skins out before chopping the nuts for the recipe. Don't use the skins because they will give the cake a bitter burnt flavor. Chop the nuts fine to maximize flavor and smoothness in the cake, or coarse if you prefer a crunchier cake.

RECOMMENDATIONS:
BASIC CRUMB CRUST (PAGE 46),
   MADE FROM GRAHAM
   CRACKERS
9-INCH SPRINGFORM PAN

INGREDIENTS:
2 POUNDS CREAM CHEESE
1½ CUPS GRANULATED SUGAR
1 TEASPOON VANILLA EXTRACT
4 LARGE EGGS, LIGHTLY BEATEN
¼ CUP HEAVY CREAM
1 CUP FINELY CHOPPED
   TOASTED HAZELNUTS (SEE
   NOTE)

Praline Cheesecake

RECOMMENDATIONS:
CRUMB-NUT CRUST (PAGE 48),
    MADE FROM GRAHAM
    CRACKERS AND PECANS
9-INCH SPRINGFORM PAN

INGREDIENTS:
1½ POUNDS CREAM CHEESE
1 CUP DARK BROWN SUGAR
2 TABLESPOONS ALL-PURPOSE
    FLOUR
3 LARGE EGGS
1 TEASPOON VANILLA EXTRACT
⅓ CUP CHOPPED PECANS

This is what you get when you cross a pecan pie with a cheesecake . . . and you don't have to be nuts to do it. This cake is even better when you top it with pecan halves and/or brush it with maple syrup.

1 Preheat the oven to 350 degrees.

2 In a large mixing bowl, beat together the cream cheese, sugar, and flour until smooth.

3 Add the eggs, one at a time, beating thoroughly after each.

4 Add the vanilla, and pecans and blend in.

5 Pour the mixture into the prepared crust and bake for 50 minutes. Open the oven door and allow the cake to cool to room temperature. Chill.

Marble Cheesecake

This cheesecake offers both a striking contrast in flavors and a beautiful two-color effect. You can vary these contrasts by changing the amounts of batter used to blend. For a more subtle variation, substitute your favorite specialty chocolate bar. (We tried semisweet mint chocolate, with spectacular results.)

1 Preheat the oven to 350 degrees.

2 Melt the chocolate in the top of a double boiler.

3 Meanwhile, in a large mixing bowl, beat the cream cheese until light and fluffy.

4 Slowly add ¾ cup sugar, then the eggs. Beat just until well blended. Stir in sour cream.

5 When the chocolate has melted, stir in remaining ¼ cup sugar and remove from heat.

6 Scoop out one cup of the cream cheese mixture and stir into chocolate, mixing thoroughly until color is uniform. Add another ½ to 1 cup of the cream cheese mixture, depending on color and consistency desired.

7 Deposit the chocolate batter, about ¼ cup at a time, on top of the light batter. To create the marble effect, dip a rubber spatula into the mix and draw swirls. Transfer the mixture into the baking pan.

8 Bake at 350 degrees until done, approximately 1 hour. Turn off oven, open oven door and let cool before refrigerating.

RECOMMENDATIONS:
BASIC CRUMB CRUST (PAGE 46)
9-INCH SPRINGFORM PAN

INGREDIENTS:
4 SQUARES (4 OUNCES)
    UNSWEETENED CHOCOLATE
2 POUNDS CREAM CHEESE
1 CUP GRANULATED SUGAR
4 LARGE EGGS, LIGHTLY BEATEN
1 CUP SOUR CREAM

Mocha Cheesecake

RECOMMENDATIONS:
BASIC CRUMB CRUST (PAGE 46),
  MADE FROM VANILLA WAFERS
8-INCH SPRINGFORM PAN

INGREDIENTS:
6 SQUARES (6 OUNCES)
  SEMISWEET CHOCOLATE
1½ POUNDS CREAM CHEESE
½ CUP GRANULATED SUGAR
2 LARGE EGGS
1 CUP HEAVY CREAM
⅓ CUP DOUBLE-STRENGTH
  COFFEE
1 TEASPOON VANILLA EXTRACT

If you like coffee with your cheesecake, you are going to love coffee *in* your cheesecake. The easiest way to produce the necessary double-strength coffee is to use instant coffee. That opens up all sorts of possibilities for cheesecake creativity. You may want to experiment with some of the new flavored instant coffees now sold, or even with the new instant espresso.

1 Preheat the oven to 350 degrees.

2 Melt the chocolate in the top part of a double boiler.

3 Meanwhile, in a large mixing bowl, beat together the cream cheese and the sugar until light.

4 Add the eggs, one at a time, beating thoroughly after each. Beat in the cream.

5 Pour the melted chocolate slowly into the cheese mixture and add the coffee and vanilla. Mix to blend ingredients thoroughly.

6 Pour the mixture into the prepared crust and bake for about 45 minutes, or until the edges of the cake are puffed up slightly. Cool in the oven with the door cracked open, then cool to room temperature. Chill.

Milk Chocolate Cheesecake

This cake is as good as the chocolate bar you select. Be choosy; use the best you can find. For variety, substitute other flavors of chocolate or liqueur.

1 Preheat the oven to 350 degrees.

2 Melt the chocolate in the top of a double boiler.

3 Meanwhile, beat together the cream cheese and sugar in a large mixing bowl. Beat in the eggs one at a time, mixing thoroughly after each.

4 Stir in the melted chocolate, then add the liqueur, butter, and sour cream. Blend well.

5 Pour the mixture into the prepared crust and bake for about 45 minutes. Turn off the heat and prop the oven door open. Let the cake cool to room temperature, then chill.

RECOMMENDATIONS:
BASIC CRUMB CRUST (PAGE 46)
9-INCH SPRINGFORM PAN

INGREDIENTS:
1 FIVE-OUNCE MILK CHOCOLATE
   BAR
1½ POUNDS CREAM CHEESE
⅔ CUP CONFECTIONERS' SUGAR
4 LARGE EGGS
⅓ CUP CHOCOLATE MINT
   LIQUEUR
4 TABLESPOONS BUTTER,
   MELTED
1 CUP SOUR CREAM

Dark Chocolate Cheesecake

RECOMMENDATIONS:
BASIC CRUMB CRUST (PAGE 46),
   MADE FROM VANILLA WAFERS
9-INCH SPRINGFORM PAN

INGREDIENTS:
5 SQUARES (5 OUNCES)
   SEMISWEET CHOCOLATE
1½ POUNDS CREAM CHEESE
¾ CUP GRANULATED SUGAR
3 LARGE EGGS
1 TEASPOON VANILLA EXTRACT
1 CUP SOUR CREAM

Is it cheesecake or fudge? Call it what you will, it is delicious.

1 Preheat the oven to 275 degrees.

2 Melt the chocolate in the top of a double boiler.

3 Meanwhile, in a large mixing bowl, beat the cream cheese with the sugar until the mixture is smooth and light.

4 Beat in the eggs and the vanilla.

5 Stir the melted chocolate and the sour cream into the cream-cheese mixture and blend well.

6 Pour the mixture into the prepared crust and bake for 1 hour, 15 minutes. Turn off the heat and allow the cake to cool in the oven. Chill.

Apple Bavarian Torte

This cake falls halfway between a cheesecake and a strudel and seems to combine the best qualities of both. The walnuts, we might note, enhance the cake tremendously; don't leave them out. The recipe comes to us courtesy of Adeline Brown of Southfield, Michigan.

1 Preheat the oven to 450 degrees.

2 In a large mixing bowl, combine the cream cheese, sugar, eggs, and vanilla. Mix until completely blended. Pour the mixture into the prepared crust.

3 Prepare the topping. Place the apple slices in a large bowl and add the sugar, cinnamon, and vanilla. Stir to mix well and to distribute the ingredients.

4 Layer the apple slices on top of the cheese mixture, then sprinkle the top with the walnut pieces.

5 Bake the torte for 15 minutes, then reduce the heat to 350 degrees and bake for an additional 45 minutes more. Cool to room temperature, then chill.

RECOMMENDATIONS:
TORTE CRUST (PAGE 58)
10-INCH SPRINGFORM PAN
APPLE TOPPING, AS GIVEN IN
  RECIPE

INGREDIENTS:
1 POUND CREAM CHEESE
½ CUP GRANULATED SUGAR
2 LARGE EGGS, LIGHTLY BEATEN
1 TEASPOON VANILLA EXTRACT

APPLE TOPPING:
3 MEDIUM APPLES, PEELED AND
  SLICED
¼ CUP GRANULATED SUGAR
½ TEASPOON GROUND
  CINNAMON
¼ TEASPOON VANILLA EXTRACT
¼ CUP COARSELY CHOPPED
  WALNUTS

Apricot Cheesecake

RECOMMENDATIONS:
BASIC CRUMB CRUST (PAGE 46)
9-INCH SPRINGFORM PAN

INGREDIENTS:
2 OUNCES DRIED APRICOTS
½ CUP WATER
1⅓ CUPS GRANULATED SUGAR
1½ POUNDS CREAM CHEESE
6 LARGE EGGS, SEPARATED
½ TEASPOON GRATED LEMON
  RIND
1 TABLESPOON LEMON JUICE
1 TEASPOON VANILLA EXTRACT
1 CUP HEAVY CREAM

If you have the weakness for apricots we have, you will love this one.

1 In a small saucepan, gently boil the apricots in the water until they become very soft. Then either press them through a sieve or beat vigorously until smooth. Stir in ⅓ cup sugar and set aside to cool.

2 Preheat the oven to 300 degrees.

3 In a large mixing bowl, beat the cream cheese and the remaining sugar until light and smooth. Beat in the egg yolks, lemon rind, lemon juice, vanilla, and cream until well blended.

4 Whip the egg whites until they form stiff peaks, then fold them into the cream-cheese mixture.

5 Pour about ⅓ of the mixture into the prepared crust, then spoon out ½ of the apricot purée in mounds on the cheese mixture. Carefully pour out another ⅓ of the batter and again dot with the purée. Cover with the remaining cheese mixture and bake for about 40 minutes. Let the cake cool in the oven for 1 hour, then remove it from the oven. Chill.

Chimpanzee Cheesecake

Your friends will go ape over this one. The flavor of bananas is subtle but pervasive. If you want a more pronounced banana taste, you'll have to monkey with the recipe a bit: eliminate the sour cream and/or top the cake with a layer of sliced bananas.

1 Preheat the oven to 350 degrees.

2 In a large mixing bowl, beat together the cream cheese, sugar, and lemon juice. Add the eggs, one at a time, beating thoroughly after each.

3 Stir in the sour cream and the mashed bananas and blend well.

4 Pour the mixture into the prepared crust and bake for 1 hour. Cool in the oven, with the door propped open, until the cake is at room temperature. Chill.

RECOMMENDATIONS:
BASIC CRUMB CRUST (PAGE 46)
9-INCH SPRINGFORM PAN

INGREDIENTS:
1 POUND CREAM CHEESE
¾ CUP GRANULATED SUGAR
2 TEASPOONS LEMON JUICE
4 LARGE EGGS
1 CUP SOUR CREAM
1 CUP MASHED BANANAS
   (APPROXIMATELY 3 MEDIUM
   BANANAS)

Pineapple Cheesecake

RECOMMENDATIONS:
BASIC CRUMB CRUST (PAGE 46)
9-INCH SPRINGFORM PAN
PINEAPPLE TOPPING, AS GIVEN IN
  RECIPE

INGREDIENTS:
1 CAN (20 OUNCES) CRUSHED
  PINEAPPLE
1 POUND CREAM CHEESE
⅔ CUP GRANULATED SUGAR
1 TEASPOON VANILLA EXTRACT
4 LARGE EGGS, LIGHTLY BEATEN

PINEAPPLE TOPPING:
2 CUPS SOUR CREAM
2 TABLESPOONS PINEAPPLE JUICE
  (FROM CANNED PINEAPPLE,
  ABOVE)
3 TABLESPOONS GRANULATED
  SUGAR

While we prefer unsweetened pineapple in this zesty cake, any will do; simply adjust the sugar to taste. Or, if you prefer, try thin slices of fresh pineapple. If you like, try a softer topping with more pineapple. Let the cake cool before adding the topping, then press pineapple slices into the topping. Serve chilled.

1 Preheat the oven to 375 degrees.

2 Drain the pineapple thoroughly, pressing to remove as much liquid as possible. Reserve the juice for the topping.

3 In a large mixing bowl, beat together the cream cheese, sugar, vanilla, and eggs until very smooth.

4 Add the pineapple and stir to blend.

5 Pour the mixture into the prepared crust and bake for 1 hour.

6 While the cake is baking, prepare the topping. Gently stir together the sour cream, pineapple juice, and sugar.

7 When the cake is ready, remove from the oven and increase the oven temperature to 450 degrees.

8 Pour the topping mixture over the cake and place the cake back in the oven. Bake for 5 minutes, then allow to cool in the oven with the door open slightly for 1 hour. Chill.

Pumpkin Cheesecake

This one puts ordinary cheesecake to shame. Served hot or just warmed, it's much like pumpkin pie, but much richer. Served cold, it's an unusual and delicious cheesecake. The cake will easily serve twenty people (or even thirty after a heavy Thanksgiving dinner), so for once you can have your cake and eat it too — serve it warm the first time around and enjoy the leftovers cold.

1 Preheat the oven to 425 degrees.

2 In a large mixing bowl, beat together the cream cheese, sugar, eggs, and yolks.

3 Add the flour, cinnamon, cloves, and ginger.

4 Beat in the cream and the vanilla, then add the mashed pumpkin and beat at medium speed on an electric mixer until just mixed thoroughly.

5 Pour the mixture into the prepared crust and bake for 15 minutes. Reduce the oven temperature to 275 degrees and bake for an additional hour. Turn off the heat, but leave the cake in the oven overnight to cool.

6 As indicated above, serve the cake either warm or chilled, with whipped cream.

RECOMMENDATIONS:
SHORTBREAD CRUST (PAGE 50)
10-INCH SPRINGFORM PAN

INGREDIENTS:
2½ POUNDS CREAM CHEESE
1 CUP GRANULATED SUGAR
4 LARGE EGGS, LIGHTLY BEATEN
3 EGG YOLKS, LIGHTLY BEATEN
3 TABLESPOONS ALL-PURPOSE
  FLOUR
2 TEASPOONS GROUND
  CINNAMON
1 TEASPOON GROUND CLOVES
1 TEASPOON GROUND GINGER
1 CUP HEAVY CREAM
1 TABLESPOON VANILLA EXTRACT
1 CAN (1 POUND) MASHED
  PUMPKIN

Sherry Cheesecake

RECOMMENDATIONS:
BASIC CRUMB CRUST (PAGE 46),
    MADE FROM VANILLA WAFERS
8-INCH SPRINGFORM PAN

INGREDIENTS:
1 POUND CREAM CHEESE
⅓ CUP GRANULATED SUGAR
3 LARGE EGGS
¼ CUP CREAM SHERRY
1 TEASPOON LEMON JUICE

After dinner, sherry and cheese are mellifluously molded here into a single dessert. In place of sherry, also try your favorite sweet wine or after-dinner liqueur.

1 Preheat the oven to 275 degrees.

2 In a large mixing bowl, beat together the cream cheese and sugar until light.

3 Add the eggs, one at a time, beating thoroughly after each.

4 Add the sherry and lemon juice and blend.

5 Pour the mixture into the prepared crust and bake for about 45 minutes, or until the cake is firm. Cool to room temperature in the oven. Serve chilled.

Ricotta Cheesecake

The taste and texture of ricotta cheese make this a refreshing change from the more common cream-cheese cakes.

1 Preheat the oven to 325 degrees.

2 Drain the ricotta of liquid.

3 In a large mixing bowl, beat the ricotta with the sugar until it is light and fluffy. Add the eggs, cornstarch, and almond extract.

4 Add the cream to the mixture, along with the almonds.

5 Pour the mixture into the prepared crust and bake for about 1 hour, or until done. Prop the oven door open and allow the cake to cool to room temperature. Chill.

RECOMMENDATIONS:
BASIC CRUMB CRUST (PAGE 46)
9-INCH SPRINGFORM PAN

INGREDIENTS:
4 CUPS (30 OUNCES) RICOTTA CHEESE
½ CUP GRANULATED SUGAR
4 LARGE EGGS, LIGHTLY BEATEN
1 TABLESPOON CORNSTARCH
1 TEASPOON ALMOND EXTRACT
1 CUP HEAVY CREAM
⅓ CUP FINELY CHOPPED ALMONDS

Passover Cheesecake

RECOMMENDATIONS:
BASIC CRUMB CRUST (PAGE 46),
    MADE FROM MATZO MEAL
8-INCH SPRINGFORM PAN

INGREDIENTS:
1 CUP (½ POUND) CREAMED
    COTTAGE CHEESE
½ POUND CREAM CHEESE
⅔ CUP GRANULATED SUGAR
3 LARGE EGGS, SEPARATED
1 TEASPOON GRATED LEMON
    RIND
1 TABLESPOON POTATO STARCH
1 CUP SOUR CREAM

This fairly light cheesecake sets up well and has a firm, moist texture. Don't worry, they'll never pass this one over.

1 Preheat the oven to 325 degrees.

2 Press the cottage cheese through a sieve and drain.

3 In a large mixing bowl, beat together the cottage cheese, cream cheese, sugar, and egg yolks.

4 Stir in the lemon rind, potato starch, and sour cream until just mixed.

5 Beat the egg whites until they form stiff peaks, then fold the whites into the cheese mixture.

6 Pour the mixture into the prepared crust and bake for 1 hour, or until set. Allow to cool in the oven, with the door propped open, for 1 hour. Chill.

Old World Cheesecake

Your guests will polish this one off in a hurry. It's a delightfully rich, sweet custardy cake. It isn't very tall or heavy, so it is an excellent accompaniment to a big dinner.

1 Preheat the oven to 350 degrees.

2 Press the cheese through a sieve, and drain.

3 In a large mixing bowl, beat the eggs, egg yolk, sugar, and vanilla at high speed for 5 minutes.

4 Blend the cheese with the butter, potatoes, baking powder, nutmeg, salt, and orange rind. Combine this with the egg mixture.

5 Pour the mixture into the prepared crust and bake for 45 minutes, or until set. Serve chilled.

RECOMMENDATIONS:
OLD WORLD CRUST (PAGE 61)
13 × 9 × 2-INCH BAKING DISH

INGREDIENTS:
2 CUPS (1 POUND) FARMER
   CHEESE OR RICOTTA
5 LARGE EGGS + 1 EGG YOLK
2 CUPS CONFECTIONERS' SUGAR
1½ TEASPOONS VANILLA
   EXTRACT
⅔ CUP BUTTER, MELTED
2 TABLESPOONS MASHED
   POTATOES
2 TEASPOONS BAKING POWDER
½ TEASPOON GRATED NUTMEG
½ TEASPOON SALT
1 TEASPOON GRATED ORANGE
   RIND

Low-Calorie Cheesecake

RECOMMENDATIONS:
LOW-CALORIE CRUST (PAGE 47)
9-INCH SPRINGFORM PAN

INGREDIENTS:
2 CUPS (1 POUND) LOW-FAT
    COTTAGE CHEESE
½ POUND LOW-FAT CREAM
    CHEESE
3 TABLESPOONS SKIM MILK
2 TEASPOONS VANILLA EXTRACT
1 LARGE EGG YOLK, LIGHTLY
    BEATEN
3 LARGE EGG WHITES
¼ CUP GRANULATED SUGAR

By our calculations, there are about 1,900 calories in this cheesecake, so if you cut it in ten pieces, it's only 190 calories per delectable slice. More corners could have been cut (like no cream cheese) but at a sacrifice of satisfaction (and we all know that means bigger slices taken or two slices polished off when one should do). If you dust the pan with crumbs after greasing with margarine you can avoid the better part of 600 calories in the crust.

1 Preheat the oven to 275 degrees.

2 Press the cottage cheese through a sieve and drain.

3 In a large mixing bowl, beat together the cottage cheese, cream cheese, milk, vanilla, and egg yolk until smooth and light.

4 Beat the egg whites slowly, adding the sugar gradually until the whites form stiff peaks. Fold the whites into the cheese mixture.

5 Pour the mixture into the prepared crust and bake for 1 hour. Turn off the heat and leave the cake in the oven for another hour. Chill.

Food Processor Cheesecake

This cake is fast, easy, and almost foolproof. The recipe is courtesy of Devora Disner of Detroit.

1 Preheat the oven to 350 degrees.

2 Place the steel blade in the food processor and put all the ingredients in the bowl, including the butter. Process until very smooth.

3 Pour the mixture into the prepared crust and bake for 30 minutes. Cool the cake in the oven, with the door propped open, until it is at room temperature. Chill.

RECOMMENDATIONS:
BASIC CRUMB CRUST (PAGE 46)
9-INCH SPRINGFORM PAN

INGREDIENTS:
2 TABLESPOONS BUTTER, MELTED AND COOLED
12 OUNCES CREAM CHEESE
1 CUP (½ POUND) COTTAGE CHEESE
½ CUP GRANULATED SUGAR
2 LARGE EGGS
1 TABLESPOON LEMON JUICE
1½ TEASPOONS VANILLA EXTRACT

Bonnie's Cheesecake

RECOMMENDATIONS:
NO CRUST
9-INCH SPRINGFORM PAN

INGREDIENTS:
½ CUP BUTTER
1 POUND CREAM CHEESE
2 CUPS (1 POUND) RICOTTA
4 LARGE EGGS
3 TABLESPOONS CORNSTARCH
3 TABLESPOONS ALL-PURPOSE
    FLOUR
1 TEASPOON LEMON JUICE
1 TEASPOON VANILLA EXTRACT
1½ CUPS GRANULATED SUGAR
2 CUPS YOGURT (SOUR CREAM
    MAY BE SUBSTITUTED)

Because this recipe doesn't call for whipped cream or whipped egg whites, it can easily be adapted for the food processor. But whether you make it in a food processor or with a mixer, the result is a delicious, golden crustless cheesecake. This recipe is courtesy of Bonnie Porte of Minneapolis.

1 Preheat the oven to 325 degrees. Lightly grease the springform pan.

2 In a saucepan, melt the butter, then allow to cool.

3 Meanwhile, in a large mixing bowl, beat the cream cheese until soft and fluffy, then add the ricotta and continue to mix until completely blended.

4 Slowly add the remaining ingredients, including the butter, and mix thoroughly.

5 Pour the mixture into the pan and bake for 1 hour.

6 Turn off the oven, but leave the cake in the oven, with the door closed, for 2 more hours. Remove and cool to room temperature. Refrigerate before serving.

No-Bake (Refrigerator) Cheesecakes

*I*f you happen to be living in a barren rooming house while you practice tap dancing your way to the big time, this is the chapter for you. All you need is a refrigerator, or just some winter weather (if things are really tough).

For those of us in more fortunate circumstances, these cakes are great for those hot, sticky summer days when you wouldn't dream of turning on the oven. Whip up a light, cool, creamy cheesecake. No sweat!

Classic No-Bake Cheesecake

RECOMMENDATIONS:
BASIC CRUMB CRUST (PAGE 46)
9-INCH SPRINGFORM PAN

INGREDIENTS:
3 CUPS (1½ POUNDS) COTTAGE
 CHEESE
2 ENVELOPES UNFLAVORED
 GELATIN
⅔ CUP GRANULATED SUGAR
¼ TEASPOON SALT
2 LARGE EGGS, SEPARATED
1 CUP MILK
1 TEASPOON GRATED LEMON
 RIND
2 TABLESPOONS LEMON JUICE
1 TEASPOON VANILLA EXTRACT
2 TABLESPOONS
 CONFECTIONERS' SUGAR
¼ TEASPOON CREAM OF TARTAR
1 CUP HEAVY CREAM

This classic recipe has been around in various versions for years. The cottage cheese, egg whites, and whipped cream make it light. Although it takes a little longer to prepare than some of the others, it is well worth the time.

1 Press the cottage cheese through a sieve and drain.

2 Mix the gelatin, sugar, and salt in a saucepan, then gently beat in the egg yolks and milk. Bring to a boil over medium heat, stirring constantly. Remove from the heat.

3 Stir the lemon rind, lemon juice, and vanilla into the gelatin mixture and allow to cool.

4 Place the cottage cheese in a large mixing bowl and add the cooled gelatin. Chill, stirring occasionally until the mixture mounds slightly when dropped from a spoon.

5 Beat the egg whites until they form soft peaks, then gradually add the sugar and cream of tartar, beating until the whites form stiff peaks. Fold the whites into the cheese mixture.

6 Whip the cream until it is stiff but not dry. Fold it into the cheese mixture.

7 Pour the mixture into the prepared crust and chill for 4 hours, or until set.

Holiday Cranberry Cheese Pie

Quackerdoodle Cheesecake

This light, cool cake has the consistency of chiffon, and it is so easy to eat.

1 Press the cottage cheese through a sieve, then beat together with the cream cheese until smooth.

2 Add the sugar and vanilla and blend well.

3 Place the gelatin and milk in a small saucepan over low heat and stir to dissolve. Remove from heat and gradually beat into the cheese mixture.

4 Beat the egg whites until they form soft peaks, then fold them into the cheese mixture.

5 Gently pour the mixture into the prepared crust, then refrigerate for 4 hours, or until set.

RECOMMENDATIONS:
BASIC CRUMB CRUST (PAGE 46), MADE FROM DIGESTIVE BISCUITS
9-INCH SPRINGFORM PAN

INGREDIENTS:
1 CUP (½ POUND) COTTAGE CHEESE
½ POUND CREAM CHEESE
½ CUP CONFECTIONERS' SUGAR
1 TEASPOON VANILLA EXTRACT
1 ENVELOPE UNFLAVORED GELATIN
1 CUP MILK
3 EGG WHITES

Egg Nog Cheesecake

RECOMMENDATIONS:
BASIC CRUMB CRUST (PAGE 46),
    MADE FROM VANILLA WAFERS
9-INCH SPRINGFORM PAN

INGREDIENTS:
2 ENVELOPES UNFLAVORED
    GELATIN
1¼ CUPS EGG NOG
4 CUPS (2 POUNDS) CREAMED
    COTTAGE CHEESE
3 LARGE EGGS, SEPARATED
½ CUP GRANULATED SUGAR
1 CUP HEAVY CREAM

You'll find that this favorite at Christmas gatherings complements your traditional egg nog recipe and earns compliments for you. The potency is up to your judgment of course.

1 Dissolve the gelatin in ¼ cup egg nog. Set aside.

2 Press the cottage cheese through a sieve. Set aside.

3 In the top of a double boiler, beat together the egg yolks and sugar. Stir in the remaining egg nog and cook gently until the mixture thickens slightly. Remove from the heat and add the gelatin mixture.

4 Place the cottage cheese in a large mixing bowl and add the gelatin mixture. Blend thoroughly.

5 Beat the egg whites until they form soft peaks, then fold into the cheese mixture.

6 Whip the cream until stiff but not dry and fold this into the cheese mixture.

7 Pour the mixture into the prepared crust and chill for 4 hours, or until set.

A Trifling Cheesecake

If you like trifle, you'll like our cheesy revision of this old favorite. The jam and the sherry are a good combination, but also try fresh fruit, slivered almonds, or your favorite jam.

1 In the top of a double boiler, place the sugar, cornstarch, and salt, then add the milk and eggs. Over medium heat, mix thoroughly until there are no lumps. Continue stirring until the mixture thickens. Remove from the heat and set aside.

2 In a large mixing bowl, beat the cream cheese and vanilla until smooth and soft. Slowly add the reserved pudding mixture, beating slowly until the cheese-and-pudding mixture is smooth.

3 Pour the mixture into the prepared crust and chill until set, about 4 hours. Serve chilled, with whipped cream.

RECOMMENDATIONS:
TRIFLE CRUST (PAGE 59)
2-QUART RECTANGULAR BAKING
 DISH

INGREDIENTS:
⅓ CUP GRANULATED SUGAR
1 TABLESPOON CORNSTARCH
¼ TEASPOON SALT
1 CUP MILK
3 LARGE EGGS, LIGHTLY BEATEN
½ POUND CREAM CHEESE
½ TEASPOON VANILLA EXTRACT

Mocha No-Bake Cheesecake

RECOMMENDATIONS:
MOCHA CRUMB CRUST (PAGE 48)
9-INCH SPRINGFORM PAN

INGREDIENTS:
1 ENVELOPE UNFLAVORED
   GELATIN
¾ CUP MILK
3 LARGE EGGS, SEPARATED
1 TABLESPOON INSTANT COFFEE
   POWDER
1 POUND CREAM CHEESE
⅓ CUP GRANULATED SUGAR
1 TEASPOON VANILLA EXTRACT
¼ CUP CONFECTIONERS' SUGAR

This is a perfect dessert for people who like a little coffee in their milk. As with the baked Mocha Cheesecake, you can experiment with a wide variety of new, flavored instant coffees. If you are a real purist, though, skip the milk and instant coffee, and use one-fourth cup of double-strength coffee instead.

1 Soften the gelatin in ¼ cup milk and set aside.

2 In the top of a double boiler, combine the egg yolks, remaining milk, and coffee. Cook, stirring, until the mixture thickens. Remove from the heat. Add the gelatin and stir until smooth.

3 In a large mixing bowl, beat the cream cheese, sugar, and vanilla until light and fluffy. Stir in the gelatin mixture.

4 Beat the egg whites until they form soft peaks, then gradually add the sugar, beating until a meringue is formed. Fold the whites into the cheese mixture.

5 Gently pour the mixture into the prepared crust and chill overnight, or until set.

Ginger No-Bake Cheesecake

For this cake, try adding more candied ginger or using ginger snaps for your crust.

1 Beat the cream cheese with the brown sugar until the mixture is light and smooth. Add the ginger and the rum and blend.

2 Place the gelatin and milk in a saucepan and heat, mixing to dissolve the gelatin. Gently beat in the egg yolks and then bring the mixture to a low boil over medium heat, stirring constantly. Remove the pot from the heat and cool.

3 When cooled, add the gelatin mixture to the cream-cheese mixture, slowly beating to mix well.

4 Pour the mixture into the prepared crust.

5 Beat the egg whites until they form soft peaks, then gradually add the confectioners' sugar and beat until the mixture is glossy.

6 Whip the cream until stiff, then stir in the rum. Fold in the egg whites.

7 Gently pour the topping over the filling and refrigerate the cake for 4 hours, or until set.

RECOMMENDATIONS:
BASIC CRUMB CRUST (PAGE 46)
9-INCH SPRINGFORM PAN
FLAVORED-CREAM TOPPING, AS
 GIVEN IN RECIPE

INGREDIENTS:
1 POUND CREAM CHEESE
½ CUP LIGHT BROWN SUGAR
2 TABLESPOONS CHOPPED
 CANDIED GINGER
2 TABLESPOONS DARK RUM
 (OPTIONAL)
1 ENVELOPE UNFLAVORED
 GELATIN
1 CUP MILK
2 LARGE EGG YOLKS

FLAVORED-CREAM TOPPING:
2 LARGE EGG WHITES
1 TABLESPOON
 CONFECTIONERS' SUGAR
1 CUP HEAVY CREAM
1 TEASPOON DARK RUM

Cider Cheesecake

RECOMMENDATIONS:
FLAVORED CRUMB CRUST
(PAGE 47), MADE WITH
CINNAMON
9-INCH SPRINGFORM PAN

INGREDIENTS:
1 CUP APPLE CIDER
2 LARGE EGGS, SEPARATED
1 ENVELOPE GELATIN
1 POUND CREAM CHEESE
½ CUP CONFECTIONERS' SUGAR
1 CUP HEAVY CREAM
1 CUP APPLE SAUCE
½ TEASPOON GROUND
CINNAMON

What could be better than apple pie and a wedge of cheese? Try this fall favorite and find out.

1 In a small saucepan, boil the cider rapidly until it is reduced by ½. Remove from the heat, then gently beat in the egg yolks. Add the gelatin and stir to dissolve.

2 In a large bowl, beat together the cream cheese and the sugar until light. Slowly add the gelatin mixture and beat until blended well.

3 Whip the cream until stiff, then stir into the batter.

4 Beat the egg whites until they form soft peaks, then fold them into the cheese mixture.

5 Stir together the apple sauce and cinnamon, then swirl into the batter.

6 Pour the mixture into the prepared crust and refrigerate for 4 hours, or until set.

No-Bake Banana Cheesecake

A tall, light, somewhat grainy cake, perfect on a hot summer day. It's only mildly sweet, but you can increase the quantity of sugar if you like. If you plan to use sliced bananas as a topping, remember that a drop of lemon juice will help keep them from turning brown.

1 Press the cottage cheese through a sieve and drain.

2 Combine the gelatin and sugar in a saucepan.

3 Beat together the milk and egg yolks until blended, then stir into the gelatin and sugar in the saucepan. Simmer over low heat, stirring constantly until the gelatin has dissolved, then remove pan from the heat.

4 Transfer the gelatin mixture to a large mixing bowl, and add the lemon rind and lemon juice.

5 Add the cottage cheese to the bowl and beat the mixture until smooth and light.

6 Beat the egg whites until they form soft peaks, then fold the whites into the cheese mixture.

7 Gently stir in the banana slices.

8 Whip the cream until stiff, then fold the cream into the mixture to blend.

9 Pour the mixture into the prepared crust and chill until firm — for up to 3 hours or even overnight. Serve chilled, possibly decorated with frosted, diced bananas arranged on top.

RECOMMENDATIONS:
FLAVORED CRUMB CRUST (PAGE 47), MADE WITH CINNAMON
9-INCH SPRINGFORM PAN

INGREDIENTS:
3 CUPS (1½ POUNDS) COTTAGE CHEESE
2 ENVELOPES UNFLAVORED GELATIN
½ CUP GRANULATED SUGAR
½ CUP MILK
2 LARGE EGGS, SEPARATED
1 TEASPOON GRATED LEMON RIND
2 TABLESPOONS LEMON JUICE
2 MEDIUM BANANAS, SLICED
1 CUP HEAVY CREAM

Grapefruit Cheesecake

RECOMMENDATIONS:
BASIC CRUMB CRUST (PAGE 46),
   MADE FROM VANILLA WAFERS
9-INCH SPRINGFORM PAN

INGREDIENTS:
1 MEDIUM GRAPEFRUIT
1 ENVELOPE UNFLAVORED
   GELATIN
1 LARGE EGG, SEPARATED
1 LARGE EGG, LEFT WHOLE
¾ CUP GRANULATED SUGAR
1 POUND CREAM CHEESE
1 CUP HEAVY CREAM

This is the perfect way to cheat on the grapefruit diet. If you really love grapefruit, add 1 teaspoon of grated rind as well.

1 Peel the grapefruit and remove the white pith. Cut the pulp into small sections. Press the sections through a sieve to capture the liquid. Include some small bits of pulp in the liquid, but be sure you do not have any large pieces. Stir in the gelatin to dissolve.

2 Place the grapefruit juice, egg yolk, whole egg, and sugar in the top of a double boiler. Heat slowly, stirring gently until the mixture thickens. Remove from the heat and set aside.

3 In a large mixing bowl, beat the cream cheese and egg white until light and fluffy. Add the egg mixture and mix until well blended. Cool.

4 Whip the cream until slightly stiff, then fold into the cream cheese mixture.

5 Pour the mixture into the prepared crust and chill until set. Serve chilled, perhaps with grapefruit sections or a glaze.

Inscrutable Cheesecake

Who can pass up the delightful flavor and color of mandarin oranges?

1 In a large mixing bowl, beat together the cream cheese, sugar, lemon rind, and lemon juice until the mixture is light and fluffy.

2 Drain the mandarin oranges, reserving the fruit and ½ cup of juice. In a small saucepan, dissolve the gelatin in the juice. Put the saucepan over medium heat, and add the milk.

3 Carefully add the egg yolks, stirring constantly. Bring to a boil, then remove from the heat.

4 Slowly beat the gelatin mixture into the cheese mixture. Stir in the sour cream.

5 Beat the egg whites until they form soft peaks, then fold them into the cheese mixture.

6 Arrange half of the orange segments on the crust, then pour the batter over the oranges. Refrigerate the cake for 4 hours, or until set.

7 Top the cake with whipped cream and the remaining orange segments.

RECOMMENDATIONS:
BASIC CRUMB CRUST (PAGE 46)
9-INCH SPRINGFORM PAN
WHIPPED CREAM TOPPING
(PAGE 68)

INGREDIENTS:
1 POUND CREAM CHEESE
½ CUP GRANULATED SUGAR
1 TEASPOON GRATED LEMON
  RIND
1 TABLESPOON LEMON JUICE
1 CAN (11 OUNCES) MANDARIN
  ORANGE SEGMENTS, WITH
  JUICE
1 ENVELOPE UNFLAVORED
  GELATIN
½ CUP MILK
2 LARGE EGGS, SEPARATED
2 CUPS SOUR CREAM

Pineapple No-Bake Cheesecake

RECOMMENDATIONS:
BASIC CRUMB CRUST (PAGE 46)
   MADE FROM TOAST CRUMBS
9-INCH SPRINGFORM PAN

INGREDIENTS:
1 CAN (15¼ OUNCES) CRUSHED
   PINEAPPLE
2 CUPS (1 POUND) COTTAGE
   CHEESE
1 ENVELOPE UNFLAVORED
   GELATIN
½ CUP GRANULATED SUGAR
3 LARGE EGGS, SEPARATED
½ POUND CREAM CHEESE
2 TABLESPOONS LEMON JUICE
3 TABLESPOONS
   CONFECTIONERS' SUGAR
1 CUP HEAVY CREAM

The perfect antidote to a sweltering summer day, this tall, tropical beauty won't disappoint anyone.

1 Press the pineapple through a sieve to remove as much liquid as possible. Reserve the liquid.

2 Press the cottage cheese through a sieve and drain.

3 Dissolve the gelatin in ¼ cup of the reserved pineapple juice.

4 In the top of a double boiler, beat together the sugar and the egg yolks. Heat until slightly thickened, then remove from the heat. Stir in the gelatin mixture and set aside.

5 In a large mixing bowl, beat together the cottage cheese, cream cheese, and lemon juice until smooth. Slowly add the yolk-gelatin and pineapple mixture to blend.

6 Beat the egg whites until they form soft peaks, then gradually add the confectioners' sugar and continue beating until the whites form stiff peaks. Fold the egg whites into the cheese mixture.

7 Whip the cream until it is stiff, then fold it into the cheese mixture.

8 Pour the mixture into the prepared crust and chill for 4 hours, or until set.

Brandy Cheesecake

This is a gastronomic interpretation of Debussy's Three-Part Invention for Flute, Harp, and Viola. Note how the zestful exuberance of the flute and the lyric arrogance of the harp (represented here by the orange juice and orange peel, respectively) provide an articulated counterpart to the graceful sonorities of the viola (represented here by the brandy). Well, you will have your own interpretations of this beauty.

1 Dissolve the gelatin in the milk, then gently heat in a double boiler, stirring until all lumps disappear. Remove from heat and set aside.

2 In a large mixing bowl, beat the eggs and sugar until they are fluffy and lemon colored.

3 To the egg mixture, add the cream cheese, vanilla, orange rind, orange juice, and brandy. Beat together until the mixture is smooth. Slowly add the gelatin mixture to the bowl, incorporating it with the cheese.

4 Gently stir in the sour cream.

5 Pour the mixture into the prepared crust and refrigerate overnight, or until set.

RECOMMENDATIONS:
SPONGECAKE LAYER (PAGE 52), PREBAKED
9-INCH SPRINGFORM PAN

INGREDIENTS:
1 ENVELOPE UNFLAVORED GELATIN
½ CUP MILK
2 LARGE EGGS
⅓ CUP GRANULATED SUGAR
1 POUND CREAM CHEESE
1 TEASPOON VANILLA EXTRACT
1 TEASPOON GRATED ORANGE RIND
1 TABLESPOON ORANGE JUICE
3 TABLESPOONS BRANDY
1 CUP SOUR CREAM

Daiquiri Cheesecake

RECOMMENDATIONS:
BASIC CRUMB CRUST (PAGE 46),
9-INCH SPRINGFORM PAN

INGREDIENTS:
1 ENVELOPE UNFLAVORED
  GELATIN
½ CUP GRANULATED SUGAR
⅓ CUP LIGHT RUM
½ CUP LIME JUICE
1 TEASPOON GRATED LIME RIND
1 TEASPOON GRATED LEMON
  RIND
4 LARGE EGGS, SEPARATED
1 POUND CREAM CHEESE
½ CUP CONFECTIONERS' SUGAR
1 CUP HEAVY CREAM

A favorite summer drink finds a new use. If you don't have lemon or lime, try adding a package of daiquiri mix to the batter. It is delicious, too, with or without the rum (you can substitute milk if you like).

1 In a medium saucepan, or the top of a double boiler, combine the gelatin, sugar, rum, and lime juice. Stir in the grated rinds, then add the egg yolks, thoroughly mixing all ingredients. Cook the mixture over medium heat, stirring constantly until it thickens, then remove the saucepan from the heat and allow to cool.

2 In a large mixing bowl, beat the cream cheese until it is light and smooth.

3 Add the gelatin mixture to the cream cheese and mix to blend all ingredients thoroughly.

4 Beat the egg whites until they form soft peaks, then slowly add the sugar and continue beating until they form stiff peaks. Fold the whites into the cream-cheese mixture.

5 Whip the cream until it is stiff, then fold it into the cheese mixture.

6 Pour the mixture into the prepared crust and chill for 4 hours, or until set.

Frozen Cheesecake

If you like ice cream, and you like cheesecake, you'll probably be tempted by this unusual frozen cheesecake. It is easy to prepare, and it will keep practically forever. Once frozen, it is best kept covered with plastic wrap. This recipe is courtesy of Lee Fidge of Detroit.

1 Place the cottage cheese in a sieve and drain.

2 In a large mixing bowl, beat together the cottage cheese and the cream cheese. Add the sugar and blend until smooth and light.

3 Add the egg yolks, salt, and vanilla and blend thoroughly.

4 Beat the egg whites until they form soft peaks, then gently fold them into the cream-cheese mixture.

5 Whip the cream until it is stiff and fold into the batter.

6 Pour the mixture into the prepared crust. Place the cake in the freezer for 4 hours, or until frozen solid. Serve frozen.

RECOMMENDATIONS:
BASIC CRUMB CRUST (PAGE 46)
9-INCH SPRINGFORM PAN

INGREDIENTS:
1 CUP (½ POUND) COTTAGE
  CHEESE
½ POUND CREAM CHEESE
1 CUP GRANULATED SUGAR
3 LARGE EGGS, SEPARATED
½ TEASPOON SALT
½ TEASPOON VANILLA EXTRACT
1 CUP HEAVY CREAM

Cheese Pies

Aunt Anita's Cheesecake

What can we say? It's true. Cheese pies are sawed off cheesecakes — lesser versions of the classic things. They are mere pies. But then again, small is beautiful; pie isn't so bad; and who ever heard of lemon meringue cake?

Basic Cheese Pie

RECOMMENDATIONS:
NUT CRUST (PAGE 49), PREBAKED
9-INCH PIE PAN

INGREDIENTS:
½ POUND CREAM CHEESE
½ CUP GRANULATED SUGAR
1 CAN (13 OUNCES) EVAPORATED
    MILK
2 LARGE EGGS
2 TABLESPOONS LEMON JUICE
1 TEASPOON VANILLA EXTRACT

This is one of the easiest recipes to make and it results in a moist, creamy pie which tastes as cheesy as the best of them.

1 Preheat the oven to 350 degrees.

2 In a large mixing bowl, beat the cream cheese until light and fluffy.

3 Slowly add the sugar, evaporated milk, eggs, lemon juice, and vanilla. Beat until light and smooth.

4 Pour the mixture into the prepared crust and bake for about 30 minutes, or until set. Cool to room temperature, then serve chilled.

Margaret's Never-Fail Cheese Pie

This may remind you of your favorite dairy-case brand, but this pie is a lot better.

1 Preheat the oven to 375 degrees.

2 In a large mixing bowl, beat together the cream cheese, sugar, eggs, and vanilla.

3 Pour the mixture into the prepared crust and bake for 20 minutes.

4 Meanwhile, prepare the topping, following the directions given with the recipe.

5 Spread the topping over the pie and return it to the oven for 5 minutes. Remove from the oven and allow to cool, then chill.

RECOMMENDATIONS:
BASIC CRUMB CRUST (PAGE 46)
9-INCH PIE PAN
SOUR-CREAM TOPPING (PAGE 68)

INGREDIENTS:
¾ POUND CREAM CHEESE
½ CUP GRANULATED SUGAR
2 LARGE EGGS, LIGHTLY BEATEN
1 TABLESPOON VANILLA EXTRACT

Honey Cheese Pie

RECOMMENDATIONS:
BASIC PASTRY PIE CRUST
(PAGE 54), PREBAKED
9-INCH PIE PAN

INGREDIENTS:
1½ CUPS (12 OUNCES) COTTAGE
CHEESE
¼ CUP HONEY
½ CUP GRANULATED SUGAR
3 LARGE EGGS, LIGHTLY BEATEN
1 TEASPOON GROUND
CINNAMON

Not too heavy, not too rich, this custardy cheese pie is an all-around treat.

1 Preheat the oven to 350 degrees.

2 Press the cottage cheese through a sieve.

3 In a large mixing bowl, combine the cottage cheese with the honey and sugar and beat until smooth.

4 Add the eggs and blend in the cinnamon.

5 Pour the mixture into the prepared crust and bake for 20 minutes, or until set. Cool to room temperature, then chill.

No-Bake Honey Cheese Pie

The flavor of honey permeates this light, cool beauty. Try using specialty honeys (like orange blossom) for an added dimension. The flavors seem to meld better with time, so leftovers may be even better than the first time around.

1 Press the cottage cheese through a sieve. Set aside.

2 In the top of a double boiler, stir together the honey, gelatin, egg yolk, and milk and cook over medium heat, stirring constantly, until the mixture is thickened slightly. Remove from the heat.

3 In a large mixing bowl, beat together the cottage cheese, cream cheese, lemon rind, and lemon juice. When smooth, add the gelatin mixture and then chill until mounds form when dropped from a spoon.

4 Beat the egg whites until they form stiff peaks, then fold the whites into the cheese mixture.

5 Whip the cream until it is stiff, then fold into the cheese mixture.

6 Pour the mixture into the prepared crust and chill for 4 hours, or until set.

RECOMMENDATIONS:
BASIC CRUMB CRUST (PAGE 46)
9-INCH PIE PAN

INGREDIENTS:
1 CUP COTTAGE CHEESE
½ CUP HONEY
1 ENVELOPE UNFLAVORED
  GELATIN
1 LARGE EGG, SEPARATED
½ CUP MILK
½ POUND CREAM CHEESE
1 TEASPOON GRATED LEMON
  RIND
1 TABLESPOON LEMON JUICE
½ CUP HEAVY CREAM

Buttermilk Cottage-Cheese Pie

RECOMMENDATIONS:
BASIC PASTRY PIE CRUST
   (PAGE 54), PREBAKED
9-INCH PIE PAN

INGREDIENTS:
1 CUP (½ POUND) COTTAGE
   CHEESE
3 TABLESPOONS ALL-PURPOSE
   FLOUR
½ CUP GRANULATED SUGAR
¼ TEASPOON SALT
3 LARGE EGGS, SEPARATED
4 TABLESPOONS BUTTER,
   MELTED
1 CUP BUTTERMILK
1 TEASPOON VANILLA EXTRACT
1 TEASPOON GRATED LEMON
   RIND
3 TABLESPOONS
   CONFECTIONERS' SUGAR

A different combination: butter, buttermilk, and cottage cheese team up to make a dairyman's delight. This is a pie that is rich but not heavy, with just a hint of the tang of buttermilk.

1 Preheat the oven to 450 degrees.

2 Press the cottage cheese through a sieve.

3 Combine the flour, sugar, and salt and set aside.

4 In a large mixing bowl, blend the egg yolks and butter. Add the cottage cheese, buttermilk, vanilla, and lemon rind and beat thoroughly.

5 Add the dry mixture and mix thoroughly.

6 Beat the egg whites until they form soft peaks, then gradually add the sugar, beating until the whites form stiff peaks. Fold the whites into the cheese mixture.

7 Pour the mixture into the prepared crust and bake for 15 minutes. Reduce the oven temperature to 350 degrees, and bake for 30 additional minutes, or until a knife comes out clean. Remove the pie from the oven and allow to cool to room temperature. Serve at room temperature.

Chocolate Cheese Pie

Coffee and chocolate really do bring out the best in each other, but if you prefer the taste of chocolate by itself, simply substitute milk for the coffee in this recipe.

1 Melt the chocolate in the top of a double boiler. Cool slightly.

2 Soften the gelatin in the coffee.

3 In a large mixing bowl, beat together the cream cheese, sugar, and vanilla until the mixture is smooth. Add the egg yolks, one at a time, beating after each.

4 Beat in the chocolate, then add the gelatin mixture.

5 Beat the egg whites until they form soft peaks, then gradually add the sugar, beating until the whites form stiff peaks. Fold the whites into the cheese mixture.

6 Whip the cream until it is semifirm, then fold it into the cheese mixture.

7 Gently pour the mixture into the prepared crust, and chill for 4 hours, or until set. Serve the pie chilled, topped with whipped cream and chocolate curls.

RECOMMENDATIONS:
CHOCOLATE CRUMB CRUST
  (PAGE 48)
9-INCH PIE PAN

INGREDIENTS:
6 SQUARES (6 OUNCES)
  SEMISWEET CHOCOLATE
1 TEASPOON UNFLAVORED
  GELATIN
¼ CUP STRONG COFFEE,
  WARMED
½ POUND CREAM CHEESE
½ CUP GRANULATED SUGAR
1 TEASPOON VANILLA EXTRACT
2 LARGE EGGS, SEPARATED
2 TABLESPOONS
  CONFECTIONERS' SUGAR
1 CUP HEAVY CREAM

Blue-Bottom Pie

RECOMMENDATIONS:
SIMPLE FRUIT CRUST (PAGE 63),
    MADE WITH BLUEBERRIES
9-INCH PIE PAN

Ah, blueberry season and what could be better than blueberries and cream? Blueberries and cream cheese! A perfect combination.

Be sure to coat the pie pan generously with butter to make it easier to remove the pie. If you can manage it (it takes three hands), this makes a very striking upside-down pie.

INGREDIENTS:
1 CUP (½ POUND) COTTAGE
    CHEESE
1 ENVELOPE UNFLAVORED
    GELATIN
⅓ CUP GRANULATED SUGAR
1 LARGE EGG, SEPARATED
1 CUP HEAVY CREAM
½ POUND CREAM CHEESE
½ TEASPOON GRATED LEMON
    RIND
1 TABLESPOON LEMON JUICE

1 Press the cottage cheese through a sieve. Set aside.

2 In the top of a double boiler, mix the gelatin and sugar, then stir in the egg yolk and half the cream. Blend thoroughly. Cook over medium heat, stirring constantly, until gelatin dissolves. Remove from the heat.

3 In a large mixing bowl, beat the cottage cheese and cream cheese with the lemon rind and lemon juice until light and fluffy.

4 Stir in the gelatin mixture and chill until thickened slightly.

5 Beat the egg white until it forms stiff peaks, then fold it into the cheese mixture.

6 Whip the remaining cream until stiff, then fold into the cheese mixture.

7 Pour the mixture into the prepared crust and chill for 4 hours, or until set.

Holiday Cranberry Cheese Pie

This colorful beauty will brighten up a few faces at any holiday feast. Try making your own cranberry sauce; it's even better.

1 Preheat the oven to 375 degrees.

2 In a large mixing bowl, beat the cream cheese until it is light, then add the eggs.

3 Gradually add the sugar and vanilla, beating until the mixture is fluffy.

4 Stir in the sour cream.

5 Pour the mixture into the prepared crust and bake for 30 minutes, or until center is firm. Cool to room temperature.

6 Prepare the topping. Place all ingredients in a large saucepan over moderate heat. Stir constantly until the mixture thickens, about 5 minutes.

7 Allow to cool, then spread over the pie just before serving. Serve the pie chilled.

RECOMMENDATIONS:
BASIC CRUMB CRUST (PAGE 46)
9-INCH PIE PAN
CRANBERRY TOPPING, AS GIVEN
   IN RECIPE

INGREDIENTS:
¾ POUND CREAM CHEESE
2 LARGE EGGS, LIGHTLY BEATEN
½ CUP GRANULATED SUGAR
1 TEASPOON VANILLA EXTRACT
2 CUPS SOUR CREAM

CRANBERRY TOPPING:
2 CUPS WHOLE BERRY
   CRANBERRY SAUCE
1 TABLESPOON CORNSTARCH
3 TABLESPOONS GRANULATED
   SUGAR
½ TEASPOON GRATED ORANGE
   RIND

Hawaiian Cheese Pie

RECOMMENDATIONS:
BASIC PASTRY PIE CRUST
   (PAGE 54), PREBAKED
9-INCH PIE PAN

INGREDIENTS:
1 CAN (15 OUNCES)
   UNSWEETENED CRUSHED
   PINEAPPLE
¼ CUP BROWN SUGAR
½ POUND CREAM CHEESE
4 TABLESPOONS BUTTER
1 CUP GRANULATED SUGAR
½ CUP SIFTED ALL-PURPOSE
   FLOUR
2 LARGE EGGS
½ CUP MILK
1 TEASPOON VANILLA EXTRACT

The light, inviting flavor of pineapple enlivens this sweet, firm cheese pie.

1 Preheat the oven to 425 degrees.

2 Drain the pineapple in a sieve; press gently to remove as much liquid as possible.

3 In a small mixing bowl, stir together the pineapple and brown sugar, then spread the mixture over the bottom of the prepared crust.

4 In a large mixing bowl, beat together the cream cheese, butter, and sugar until light. Add the flour, eggs, milk, and vanilla and beat until smooth.

5 Pour the cheese mixture over the pineapple in the crust and bake for 10 minutes. Reduce the temperature to 350 degrees and continue baking for about 30 minutes more.

6 Remove the pie from the oven and cool. Chill.

Lemon Meringue Cheese Pie

If you like lemon meringue pie and you like cheesecake, you'll love this one. Who'd believe you could improve on lemon meringue? If you've never made a meringue before, you'll be amazed at how easy it is.

1 Preheat the oven to 400 degrees.

2 In a large mixing bowl, beat together the cream cheese, egg yolks, and lemon juice until light and fluffy. Set aside.

3 In a saucepan or the top of a double boiler, place the water, sugar, cornstarch, and lemon rind. Cook over medium heat, stirring constantly, until the mixture thickens. Bring to a boil for 1 minute.

4 Slowly add the cheese mixture, stirring together until well blended (do not beat).

5 Pour the hot mixture into the prepared crust.

6 Prepare the meringue topping. Beat the egg whites with the cream of tartar until they are foamy, then add the sugar gradually until the whites form stiff peaks. Quickly add the vanilla.

7 Spread the meringue over the filling, making sure that you seal it to the edges of the crust.

8 Bake the pie for 10 minutes, or until the meringue is light brown. Cool to room temperature, then serve.

RECOMMENDATIONS:
BASIC PASTRY PIE CRUST
 (PAGE 54), PREBAKED
9-INCH PIE PAN
MERINGUE TOPPING, AS GIVEN
 IN RECIPE

INGREDIENTS:
½ POUND CREAM CHEESE
3 EGG YOLKS
½ CUP LEMON JUICE
1 CUP WATER
1½ CUPS GRANULATED SUGAR
⅓ CUP CORNSTARCH
2 TEASPOONS GRATED LEMON
 RIND

MERINGUE TOPPING:
2 EGG WHITES
¼ TEASPOON CREAM OF TARTAR
6 TABLESPOONS
 CONFECTIONERS' SUGAR
½ TEASPOON VANILLA EXTRACT

Cream-Cheese Pie with Liqueur

RECOMMENDATIONS:
BASIC CRUMB CRUST (PAGE 46)
9-INCH PIE PAN
SOUR-CREAM TOPPING, AS GIVEN
    IN RECIPE

INGREDIENTS:
½ POUND CREAM CHEESE
½ CUP GRANULATED SUGAR
1 TEASPOON LEMON JUICE
2 LARGE EGGS, LIGHTLY BEATEN

SOUR-CREAM TOPPING:
2 CUPS SOUR CREAM
2 TABLESPOONS
    CONFECTIONERS' SUGAR
1 TABLESPOON LIQUEUR

Virtually any after-dinner liqueur will work in this recipe, but orange-flavored liqueurs are particularly good. For an added touch, lightly press mandarin orange sections into the sour-cream topping. Properly set, this pie is creamy but firm, easy to slice, and especially easy to eat.

1 Preheat the oven to 375 degrees.

2 In a large mixing bowl, beat together the cream cheese, sugar, and lemon juice until light and fluffy.

3 Add the eggs and beat until smooth.

4 Pour the mixture into the prepared crust and bake for 20 minutes. Allow to cool for 30 minutes.

5 While the pie is cooling, prepare the sour-cream topping. Blend the sour cream with the sugar and the liqueur, but do not beat the ingredients.

6 When the pie is cool, pour the topping over the pie and bake for 5 to 7 minutes in a 450-degree oven. Remove from the oven and chill before serving.

Oobleck Pie (Avocado Cheese Pie)

This recipe comes to us from Win Bowron of Berkeley, California. Win has reportedly made this one on camping trips. It will win no beauty contests, but if you like avocados, you will also like this cheesecake.

1 Preheat the oven to 350 degrees.

2 In a large mixing bowl, beat together the avocados, lime juice, cream cheese, and egg white until ingredients are well blended.

3 Add the honey and blend until thoroughly mixed.

4 Pour the mixture into the prepared crust and bake for 20 to 25 minutes, or until done. Allow to cool.

5 Sprinkle wheat germ on top and serve chilled.

RECOMMENDATIONS:
CRUMB-NUT CRUST (PAGE 48),
    MADE WITH WALNUTS
10-INCH PIE PAN

INGREDIENTS:
3 MEDIUM, RIPE AVOCADOS,
    PEELED AND SEEDS REMOVED
5 TABLESPOONS LIME JUICE
1 POUND CREAM CHEESE
1 EGG WHITE
¾ CUP HONEY
WHEAT GERM

Tofu Pie

RECOMMENDATIONS:
WHOLE-WHEAT PIE CRUST
(PAGE 56), PREBAKED
9-INCH PIE PAN

INGREDIENTS:
1½ CUPS SOFT TOFU
4 TABLESPOONS DRY MILK
POWDER
2 LARGE EGGS, LIGHTLY BEATEN
¾ CUP HONEY
¼ TEASPOON SALT
1 TEASPOON GROUND
CINNAMON
½ TEASPOON GROUND GINGER
¾ TEASPOON GRATED NUTMEG
¾ CUP MILK

This isn't really a cheesecake or pie, of course, but we think it is so interesting and unusual that we decided to include it anyway. Tofu, also known as bean curd or soybean cheese, can be found in many health food stores and Oriental groceries. This recipe is courtesy of Grace Niedbala of Detroit.

1 Preheat the oven to 450 degrees.

2 In a large mixing bowl, combine all the ingredients for the filling and blend together until smooth.

3 Pour the mixture into the prepared crust and bake for 15 minutes. Reduce the heat to 350 degrees and bake for 30 minutes more, or until a knife comes out clean. Allow to cool before serving.

Cottage-Cheese Cakes

Italian Cheesecake

$\mathcal{C}$ream cheese has no hegemony over the cheesecake world. In fact, it's an upstart. Before its invention in 1872, fresh curd (similar to cottage cheese) was the cheese of choice. And those old timers knew a good thing. Cottage-cheese cakes, while slightly less creamy, are generally less heavy than cream-cheese cakes. Half-and-half combinations of cream cheese and cottage cheese are the best of both. We think the combination must be the most fortunate pairing since Mae West met W. C. Fields. Give them a try!

Note: A few of these recipes use homemade curd, but any of these cottage-cheese cakes could use this homemade variety. Try it.

The Hybrid

RECOMMENDATIONS:
BASIC CRUMB CRUST (PAGE 46)
9-INCH SPRINGFORM PAN

The traditional cheesecakes of Central and Eastern Europe have always been made with cottage cheese and such variants as farmer cheese. French cheesecakes occasionally call for cheeses with a higher butterfat content, but the rich, creamy cakes that we know are essentially American. This cheesecake is a compromise between these traditions, and we think a happy one.

INGREDIENTS:
2 CUPS (1 POUND) SMALL-CURD
   COTTAGE CHEESE
1 POUND CREAM CHEESE
1 CUP GRANULATED SUGAR
1 TEASPOON GRATED LEMON
   RIND
1 TEASPOON LEMON JUICE
1 TEASPOON VANILLA EXTRACT
1 TABLESPOON CORNSTARCH
6 LARGE EGGS
2 CUPS SOUR CREAM

1 Preheat the oven to 325 degrees.

2 Press the cottage cheese through a sieve.

3 In a large mixing bowl, place the cottage cheese and cream cheese and beat until light and fluffy.

4 Gradually add the sugar, lemon rind, lemon juice, vanilla, and cornstarch.

5 Add the eggs, one at a time, beating thoroughly after each.

6 Add the sour cream and beat just until smooth.

7 Pour the mixture into the prepared crust and bake for 1½ hours. Cool in the oven for 2 hours, then chill.

Basic Cottage-Cheese Cake

If you are accustomed to the richer, creamier cream-cheese cakes, this one may take a little getting used to. If it strikes you as a little bland, one way to liven it up is to put a layer of dried apricots, stewed and drained, into the crust before adding the cheese mixture.

1 Preheat the oven to 275 degrees.

2 Press the cottage cheese through a sieve.

3 In a large mixing bowl, beat the cottage cheese until smooth.

4 Add the sugar and the eggs while beating steadily at medium speed.

5 Beat in the lemon rind, lemon juice, nutmeg, and flour.

6 Add the vanilla to the cream and whip the cream until it is stiff. Fold the cream into the cheese mixture.

7 Pour the mixture into the prepared crust and bake for 1½ hours or until set. Turn off the oven and leave the cake in the oven for another hour. Cool to room temperature. Chill before serving.

RECOMMENDATIONS:
CRUMB-NUT CRUST (PAGE 48),
    FLAVORED WITH CINNAMON
9-INCH SPRINGFORM PAN

INGREDIENTS:
2 CUPS (1 POUND) CREAMED
    COTTAGE CHEESE
1 CUP GRANULATED SUGAR
3 LARGE EGGS
1 TEASPOON GRATED LEMON
    RIND
2 TEASPOONS LEMON JUICE
½ TEASPOON GRATED NUTMEG
½ CUP SIFTED ALL-PURPOSE
    FLOUR
1 TEASPOON VANILLA EXTRACT
1 CUP HEAVY CREAM

Buttery Cheesecake

RECOMMENDATIONS:
CRUMB-NUT CRUST (PAGE 48)
9-INCH SPRINGFORM PAN

INGREDIENTS:
4 CUPS (2 POUNDS) COTTAGE
  CHEESE
3 TABLESPOONS BUTTER,
  MELTED
¼ CUP GRANULATED SUGAR
4 LARGE EGGS
¼ CUP ALL-PURPOSE FLOUR
1 TEASPOON VANILLA EXTRACT

The melted butter in this cake gives it a richness (and butterfat content) comparable to many of the cream-cheese cakes, but it retains the lighter, grainier texture of the cottage-cheese cakes.

1 Preheat the oven to 300 degrees.

2 Press the cottage cheese through a sieve.

3 In a large mixing bowl, beat the cottage cheese until smooth.

4 Add the butter, sugar, and eggs and blend.

5 Mix in the flour and vanilla until well blended.

6 Pour the mixture into the prepared crust and bake for 1½ hours. Cool to room temperature, then chill.

Sour-Cream Cheesecake

There's something refreshing in the taste of sour cream, as you can taste with your first bite of this tangy, light cheesecake.

1 Preheat the oven to 325 degrees.

2 Press the cottage cheese through a sieve.

3 In a large mixing bowl, beat together the cottage cheese and cream cheese until light and smooth.

4 Add the egg yolks, cornstarch, and sugar and blend.

5 Stir in the lemon rind and sour cream and mix well.

6 Beat the egg whites until they form stiff peaks, then fold them into the cheese mixture.

7 Pour the mixture into the prepared crust, and bake for about 1¼ hours, or until set. Prop the oven door open and allow the cake to cool to room temperature in the oven. Chill.

RECOMMENDATIONS:
BASIC CRUMB CRUST (PAGE 46)
    MADE FROM BREAD CRUMBS
9-INCH SPRINGFORM PAN

INGREDIENTS:
2 CUPS (1 POUND) CREAMED
    COTTAGE CHEESE
½ POUND CREAM CHEESE
3 LARGE EGGS, SEPARATED
2 TABLESPOONS CORNSTARCH
¼ CUP GRANULATED SUGAR
1 TEASPOON GRATED LEMON
    RIND
2 CUPS SOUR CREAM

Westphalian Cheesecake

RECOMMENDATIONS:
SHORTBREAD CRUST (PAGE 50)
9-INCH SPRINGFORM PAN

INGREDIENTS:
1½ CUPS (12 OUNCES)
   SMALL-CURD COTTAGE
   CHEESE
6 TABLESPOONS BUTTER
¾ CUP GRANULATED SUGAR
4 LARGE EGGS, SEPARATED
½ TEASPOON VANILLA EXTRACT
8 OUNCES CREAM CHEESE
1 TEASPOON CORNSTARCH

Julia Evans of Detroit, Michigan, learned this recipe from her grandmother in Germany. Though it is perhaps less rich and sweet than many in our collection, we find this cake to be an agreeable and delicate change of pace.

1 Preheat the oven to 325 degrees.

2 Press the cottage cheese through a sieve.

3 In a large mixing bowl, cream the butter with the sugar, then add the egg yolks and vanilla. Blend until the mixture is light and fluffy.

4 Add the cream cheese, cottage cheese, and cornstarch and blend thoroughly.

5 Beat the egg whites until they form stiff peaks and then fold them into the cheese batter.

6 Pour the mixture into the prepared crust and bake for 1 hour, or until the top is golden brown. Leave the cake in the oven to cool for 2 hours, then chill.

Cheesecake Katherine

The unexpected flavor of oranges brings sunshine to this light and creamy cake. Try topping it with an arrangement of mandarin orange sections.

1 Preheat the oven to 350 degrees.

2 Press the cottage cheese through a sieve.

3 Sift together the flour and the baking powder and set aside.

4 In a large mixing bowl, beat the cottage cheese at high speed until smooth. Then add the cream cheese and the sugar and beat until light and fluffy.

5 Add the flour mixture and the orange rind, orange juice, and liqueur. Beat until thoroughly blended.

6 Add the egg yolks, one at a time, beating thoroughly after each.

7 Add the sour cream and blend well.

8 Beat the egg whites until they form stiff peaks, then fold into the cheese mixture.

9 Pour the mixture into the prepared crust and bake for 45 minutes, or until center is firm. Leave the cake in the oven to cool for 2 hours, then chill.

RECOMMENDATIONS:
CRUMB-NUT CRUST (PAGE 48)
9-INCH SPRINGFORM PAN

INGREDIENTS:
2 CUPS (1 POUND) COTTAGE
   CHEESE
¼ CUP ALL-PURPOSE FLOUR
¼ TEASPOON BAKING POWDER
½ POUND CREAM CHEESE
1 CUP GRANULATED SUGAR
1 TEASPOON GRATED ORANGE
   RIND
2 TEASPOONS ORANGE JUICE
1 TEASPOON ORANGE-FLAVORED
   LIQUEUR
5 LARGE EGGS, SEPARATED
1 CUP SOUR CREAM

Aunt Anita's Cheesecake

RECOMMENDATIONS:
SIMPLEST CRUST (PAGE 63)
9-INCH SPRINGFORM PAN

INGREDIENTS:
2 CUPS (1 POUND) SMALL-CURD
   COTTAGE CHEESE
1 POUND CREAM CHEESE
1½ CUPS GRANULATED SUGAR
4 LARGE EGGS, LIGHTLY BEATEN
¼ CUP CORNSTARCH
2 TABLESPOONS LEMON JUICE
1 TEASPOON VANILLA EXTRACT
½ CUP BUTTER, MELTED
2 CUPS SOUR CREAM

This medium-heavy, oh-so-rich cheesecake is a secret old family recipe. We can tell you the recipe, but not the family.

1 Preheat the oven to 325 degrees.

2 Press the cottage cheese through a sieve.

3 In a large mixing bowl, beat the cottage cheese and cream cheese together at high speed until creamy.

4 Add the sugar and eggs and beat until blended.

5 With the mixer set on low, add the cornstarch, lemon juice, and vanilla. Beat until smooth.

6 Add the butter and sour cream and mix until just blended.

7 Pour the mixture into the prepared crust and bake for 1 hour, 10 minutes, or until the cake is firm at the edges and slightly browned. Cool to room temperature, then chill.

Cheese Retorte

Eight eggs! Your guests will crow over this one. After a second helping, they also will sprout feathers and start laying eggs. It is extremely rich, and yet very light. As always, handle the egg whites very carefully.

1 Preheat the oven to 275 degrees.

2 Press the cottage cheese through a sieve.

3 In a large mixing bowl, beat the cottage cheese until smooth. Add the sugar and beat at medium speed to remove all lumps.

4 Beat in the egg yolks, lemon rind, and lemon juice, then add the flour, blending to mix well.

5 Whip the cream until it thickens, then stir into the cheese mixture carefully.

6 Beat the egg whites until they form soft peaks. Gently fold the whites into the cheese mixture.

7 Pour the mixture into the prepared crust and bake for 1½ hours, or until the center is firm. Turn off the oven and leave the cake in the oven to cool. Chill.

RECOMMENDATIONS:
FLAVORED CRUMB CRUST
 (PAGE 47)
10-INCH SPRINGFORM PAN

INGREDIENTS:
4 CUPS (2 POUNDS) CREAMED
 COTTAGE CHEESE
1½ CUPS GRANULATED SUGAR
8 LARGE EGGS, SEPARATED
1 TEASPOON GRATED LEMON
 RIND
2 TEASPOONS LEMON JUICE
5 TABLESPOONS ALL-PURPOSE
 FLOUR
1½ CUPS HEAVY CREAM

Fresh-Curd Cheesecake

Almost a cheese pie, this Old World cheesecake is best with a sour-cream topping.

RECOMMENDATIONS:
BASIC CRUMB CRUST (PAGE 46),
  MADE FROM DIGESTIVE
  BISCUITS
9-INCH SPRINGFORM PAN
SOUR-CREAM TOPPING, AS GIVEN
  IN RECIPE

INGREDIENTS:
2 CUPS FRESH CURD (SEE NOTE)
⅔ CUP GRANULATED SUGAR
1 TEASPOON VANILLA EXTRACT
1 TABLESPOON LEMON JUICE
4 LARGE EGGS

SOUR-CREAM TOPPING:
2 CUPS SOUR CREAM
¼ CUP GRANULATED SUGAR
2 TEASPOONS BRANDY

1 Preheat the oven to 325 degrees.

2 In a large mixing bowl, beat together the curd, sugar, vanilla, and lemon juice until light and fluffy.

3 Add the eggs, one at a time, beating thoroughly after each.

4 Pour the mixture into the prepared crust and bake for 40 minutes.

5 While the cake is baking, prepare the topping. In a mixing bowl, stir together the sour cream, sugar, and brandy until blended. When the cake is finished, pour the topping over the cake and return cake to the oven for 10 additional minutes, or until topping is set. Cool to room temperature, then chill before serving.

WORDS TO THE WISE:

This recipe could be made with freshly made curds. Use the following recipe.

2 QUARTS WHOLE MILK
¼ CUP BUTTERMILK

1 In a large mixing bowl, stir together the milk and the buttermilk. Put the bowl in a warm place, such as over the pilot light of a gas stove, for 1 to 2 days. A soft curd will form on the top of the mixture.

2 Line a colander or a large strainer with several layers of cheesecloth, then skim off the curd and drain it in the cloth for a few minutes.

3 Set the colander in a large pan and wrap the pan-colander apparatus in a large plastic bag. Set this in the refrigerator for 1½ to 2 days, or longer. Curds are then ready to use.

Almond Cottage-Cheese Cake

RECOMMENDATIONS:
BASIC CRUMB CRUST (PAGE 46)
9-INCH SPRINGFORM PAN

INGREDIENTS:
4 CUPS (2 POUNDS) COTTAGE
   CHEESE
4 LARGE EGGS
¾ CUP GRANULATED SUGAR
¼ TEASPOON SALT
1 TEASPOON ALMOND EXTRACT
1 CUP MILK
¼ CUP ALL-PURPOSE FLOUR
¼ CUP CHOPPED BLANCHED
   ALMONDS

This almond-flavored cake is a simple one to prepare and should please all your guests. The recipe was given to us by Mrs. Violet Scott of South Haven, Michigan, who suggests that you reserve some crumbs from the crust to sprinkle, along with the nuts, on top just before baking.

1 Preheat the oven to 350 degrees.

2 Press the cottage cheese through a sieve.

3 In a large mixing bowl, beat the eggs with the sugar until they are light and fluffy. Add the salt, almond extract, milk, cottage cheese, and flour and mix thoroughly.

4 Pour the mixture into the prepared crust. Sprinkle the chopped nuts on top. Bake for 1 hour, or until done. Allow to cool in the oven, with the door propped open, for 3 hours. Chill.

Cheesecakes
Around the World

Virtually every country that has cows or goats has cheese, and nearly every country that has cheese has a cheesecake. Herewith, a sampling of cheesecake recipes from around the world. In several cases, we must confess that the authenticity of the recipes is somewhat suspect. Our Danish correspondent, for example, informs us that cheesecake in any form is quite unknown in that country. The recipe, though, seemed so interesting and delicious that we were hardly inclined to let such a minor consideration stand in our way. Once you've tried these recipes, we are sure you'll understand why they are included.

Australian Cheesecake

RECOMMENDATIONS:
BASIC CRUMB CRUST (PAGE 46),
8-INCH SPRINGFORM PAN

INGREDIENTS:
1 POUND CREAM CHEESE
½ CUP GRANULATED SUGAR
3 LARGE EGGS, SEPARATED
¼ CUP ALL-PURPOSE FLOUR
1 TEASPOON GRATED LEMON
  RIND
2 TEASPOONS LEMON JUICE
1 TEASPOON VANILLA EXTRACT
½ CUP HEAVY CREAM
2 TABLESPOONS PASSION FRUIT
  PULP, MADE FROM FRESH
  FRUIT

This moist, somewhat cakelike cheesecake will stir your passions. It is even good without the passion fruit; try your favorite jam instead, or make it plain.

1 Preheat the oven to 300 degrees.

2 In a large mixing bowl, beat together the cream cheese and sugar until light and fluffy.

3 Add the egg yolks, one at a time, beating thoroughly after each.

4 Beat in the flour, lemon rind, lemon juice, and vanilla until just mixed.

5 Whip the cream until stiff. Set aside.

6 Beat the egg whites until they form stiff peaks, then fold into the cheese mixture. Fold in the reserved whipped cream.

7 Stir in the passion fruit, then pour the mixture into the prepared crust and bake for 45 minutes to 1 hour. Cool to room temperature, then chill.

Austrian Cheesecake

The raisins in this cake are essential, and you can add even more if you like. This cake sets up very well upon cooling and makes a lovely appearance.

1 Preheat the oven to 300 degrees.

2 Press the cheese through a sieve.

3 In a large mixing bowl, beat together the cheese and sugar until light.

4 Add the egg yolks, one at a time, beating after each, then add the milk, lemon rind, and vanilla.

5 Stir in the flour and blend thoroughly.

6 Beat the egg whites until they form soft peaks, then gradually add the sugar, beating until the whites form stiff peaks. Fold the whites into the cheese mixture.

7 Gently stir in the raisin bits, then pour the mixture into the prepared crust. Bake for 55 minutes, or until the center appears firm. Let the cake cool in the oven for 15 minutes, then allow to cool to room temperature.

RECOMMENDATIONS:
SHORTBREAD CRUST (PAGE 50)
9-INCH SPRINGFORM PAN

INGREDIENTS:
2 CUPS (1 POUND) COTTAGE
 CHEESE OR FARMER CHEESE
½ CUP GRANULATED SUGAR
5 LARGE EGGS, SEPARATED
½ CUP MILK
½ TEASPOON GRATED LEMON
 RIND
1 TEASPOON VANILLA EXTRACT
¾ CUP SIFTED ALL-PURPOSE
 FLOUR
¼ CUP CONFECTIONERS' SUGAR
3 TABLESPOONS FINELY
 CHOPPED GOLDEN RAISINS

Belgian Cheese Tart

RECOMMENDATIONS:
SHORTBREAD CRUST (PAGE 50)
8-INCH FLAN RING OR TART PAN

INGREDIENTS:
½ POUND CREAM CHEESE
3 TABLESPOONS
    CONFECTIONERS' SUGAR
1 TEASPOON LEMON JUICE
2 LARGE EGGS
⅔ CUP HEAVY CREAM

This is a tart rather than a cake. For a delicious golden top, brush with a beaten egg mixed with one tablespoon of confectioners' sugar before baking.

1 Preheat the oven to 350 degrees.

2 In a large mixing bowl, beat together the cheese, sugar, and lemon juice until the mixture is light and fluffy.

3 Add the eggs, one at a time, beating thoroughly after each.

4 Stir in the cream and pour the mixture into the prepared crust. Bake for 25 minutes, or until set. Cool to room temperature, then chill.

Czechoslovakian Cheesecake

The rum and raisins are unusual, but it is the yeast-dough crust that really makes this cake distinctive. We call it a cheesecake, but it is really a distant cousin to the traditional Czechoslovakian *kolachy* pastry.

1 Preheat the oven to 350 degrees.

2 Press the cottage cheese through a sieve and drain.

3 In a large mixing bowl, combine the butter, sugar, and egg yolks. Beat until foamy, then add the cornstarch, milk, rum, lemon rind, and raisins and blend thoroughly.

4 Beat the egg whites until they form soft peaks, then gently fold them into the cheese mixture.

5 Pour the mixture into the prepared crust and bake for 50 minutes, or until the edges are golden brown.

6 Cool and serve at room temperature.

RECOMMENDATIONS:
SWEET YEAST CRUST (PAGE 62)
9-INCH SPRINGFORM PAN

INGREDIENTS:
2 CUPS (1 POUND) COTTAGE
   CHEESE
¼ CUP BUTTER
1 CUP GRANULATED SUGAR
2 LARGE EGGS, SEPARATED
1 TABLESPOON CORNSTARCH
3 TABLESPOONS MILK OR HEAVY
   CREAM
1 TABLESPOON DARK RUM
½ TEASPOON GRATED LEMON
   RIND
⅓ CUP RAISINS

Danish Blue-Cheese Pie

INGREDIENTS:
2 ENVELOPES UNFLAVORED
   GELATIN
½ CUP COLD WATER
4 OUNCES CREAM CHEESE
4 OUNCES DANISH BLUE CHEESE
1 CUP HEAVY CREAM
1 POUND SEEDLESS GREEN
   GRAPES

**PUMPERNICKLE CRUMB
   CRUST:**
1 LOAF (11 OUNCES)
   THIN-SLICED PUMPERNICKLE
   BREAD
½ CUP BUTTER
¼ CUP GRANULATED SUGAR

There is no sugar in this recipe; all the sweetness comes from the grapes. We think it offers a delightful balance of sweet and tart, but if it is too tart for you, add sugar according to your taste. Because it isn't as sweet as most of the other cheesecakes, this one is great at parties or served as an appetizer.

1 First prepare the crust. Preheat the oven to 250 degrees, then dry the bread slices in the oven until they are hard enough to crumble easily (about 20 to 25 minutes). Meanwhile melt the butter.

2 Crush the bread, making about 1½ cups of crumbs. Add the butter and the sugar and mix thoroughly. Press crumbs into the pie pan.

3 Raise the oven temperature to 350 degrees and bake the crust for 15 minutes. Allow to cool before filling.

4 Then prepare the filling. In a medium-sized saucepan, combine the gelatin with the water and cook over medium heat, stirring constantly until the mixture is clear (about 6 to 8 minutes). Cool.

5 In a large mixing bowl, beat the cream cheese until smooth and light.

6 Mash the blue cheese well and combine it with the cream cheese. Pour the gelatin mixture into the bowl with the cheese and mix well.

7 Whip the cream until stiff and fold it into the cheese mixture. Pour the filling gently into the prepared crust.

8 Press the grapes upright into the pie, leaving the tops showing.

9 Chill the pie several hours, or until set.

Dutch Cheesecake

RECOMMENDATIONS:
SHORTBREAD CRUST (PAGE 50)
8-INCH TART PAN

INGREDIENTS:
2 LARGE EGGS, SEPARATED
¼ CUP + 2 TEASPOONS
　CONFECTIONERS' SUGAR
1½ CUPS GRATED GOUDA
　CHEESE
⅓ CUP LIGHT CREAM OR
　HALF-AND-HALF
¼ CUP ALL-PURPOSE FLOUR
1 TEASPOON LEMON JUICE
1 TEASPOON GRATED LEMON
　RIND
⅓ CUP GOLDEN RAISINS

They probably have never heard of this cake in The Netherlands, but who cares? If you like gouda, you will love this cheesecake, but don't leave out the raisins.

1 Preheat the oven to 350 degrees.

2 In a large mixing bowl, beat together the egg yolks and ¼ cup confectioners' sugar until well blended — about 5 minutes.

3 Beat in the cheese, cream, flour, lemon juice, lemon rind, and raisins.

4 Beat the egg whites until frothy, then gradually add the remaining sugar and continue beating until the whites form stiff peaks. Fold the egg whites into the cheese mixture.

5 Pour the cheese mixture into the prepared crust and bake for 45 minutes. Cool to room temperature, then chill.

English Cheese Pie

This cheese pie has been around in various forms since the seventeenth century, and the rosewater helps to give it the flavor of an earlier age. At first, the nutmeg and cinnamon may bring pumpkin pie to mind, but this cake is far more delicate in flavor and texture. This really is more of a custard than a cheese pie.

1 Preheat the oven to 350 degrees.

2 Press the cottage cheese through a sieve.

3 In a small saucepan, gently heat the cream and the sherry until steamy; do not allow to scorch.

4 In a mixing bowl, beat together the eggs, egg yolks, sugar, rosewater, and spices until frothy — about 5 minutes.

5 In a large mixing bowl, beat the cottage cheese until it is smooth, then add the egg mixture and blend thoroughly.

6 Add the hot cream and sherry slowly to the cheese mixture and beat until well blended.

7 Stir in the currants and pour the mixture into the prepared crust. Bake for about 30 minutes, then allow to cool. Chill, and sprinkle with cinnamon.

RECOMMENDATIONS:
BASIC PASTRY PIE CRUST
  (PAGE 54)
9-INCH PIE PAN

INGREDIENTS:
½ CUP COTTAGE CHEESE
1 CUP HEAVY CREAM
¼ CUP CREAM SHERRY
3 LARGE EGGS
2 EGG YOLKS
⅓ CUP GRANULATED SUGAR
2 TABLESPOONS ROSEWATER
½ TEASPOON GRATED NUTMEG
¼ TEASPOON GROUND
  CINNAMON
¼ CUP DRIED CURRANTS

Finnish Curd Cake

RECOMMENDATIONS:
SIMPLEST CRUST (PAGE 63)
1-QUART LOAF PAN

INGREDIENTS:
1½ TEASPOONS BAKING
   POWDER
1 CUP SIFTED ALL-PURPOSE
   FLOUR
1 CUP (½ POUND) COTTAGE
   CHEESE
2 LARGE EGGS
½ CUP BROWN SUGAR
1 TEASPOON GROUND
   CINNAMON
1 TEASPOON GROUND
   CARDAMOM
½ TEASPOON GROUND GINGER
1 TEASPOON GRATED ORANGE
   RIND
1 TEASPOON GRATED LEMON
   RIND
½ CUP BUTTER, MELTED

This is not really a cheesecake in the ordinary sense of the term; in texture and appearance it has a much closer resemblance to quick breads such as zucchini bread or banana bread. You may wish to increase the sugar — our version is only mildly sweet.

1 Preheat the oven to 325 degrees.

2 Sift together the flour and baking powder and set aside.

3 Press the cottage cheese through a sieve.

4 In a large mixing bowl, beat the eggs and sugar until they are frothy.

5 Add the cinnamon, cardamom, ginger, and fruit rinds. Add the cottage cheese and blend all ingredients thoroughly.

6 Stir in the butter, then add the dry mixture, mixing thoroughly.

7 Pour the mixture into the prepared crust and bake for 1 hour.

French Cheesecake

The smoothest, richest, creamiest melt-in-your-mouth cheesecake ever ... every bite is ecstasy. To paraphrase J. P. Morgan, if you have to ask how much it costs, you can't afford to make it, and if you have to ask how many calories it has per slice, you can't afford to eat it. French double- and triple-crèmes are available in cheese specialty shops. They cost an arm and a leg.

1 Preheat the oven to 350 degrees.

2 In a large mixing bowl, beat together the cream cheese and double-crème, then add the sugar and flour and beat thoroughly.

3 Stir in the egg yolks, sour cream, heavy cream, and vanilla.

4 Beat the egg whites until they are frothy, then gradually add the sugar and beat until the whites form stiff peaks. Fold the whites into the cheese mixture.

5 Pour the mixture into the prepared crust and bake for 45 minutes, or until center is firm. Cool to room temperature, then chill.

RECOMMENDATIONS:
SHORTBREAD CRUST (PAGE 50)
9-INCH SPRINGFORM PAN

INGREDIENTS:
1 POUND CREAM CHEESE
½ POUND SOFT DOUBLE-CRÈME FRENCH CHEESE
⅓ CUP GRANULATED SUGAR
1 TABLESPOON ALL-PURPOSE FLOUR
4 LARGE EGGS, SEPARATED
¼ CUP SOUR CREAM
¼ CUP HEAVY CREAM
1 TEASPOON VANILLA EXTRACT
1 TABLESPOON CONFECTIONERS' SUGAR

German Käsekuchen

RECOMMENDATIONS:
MUERBETEIG (PAGE 60)
9-INCH SPRINGFORM PAN

INGREDIENTS:
3 CUPS (1½ POUNDS) COTTAGE
    CHEESE
½ CUP CORNSTARCH
1 TEASPOON BAKING SODA
1 CUP GRANULATED SUGAR
4 LARGE EGGS
½ TEASPOON GRATED LEMON
    RIND
½ TEASPOON VANILLA EXTRACT
1 CUP SOUR CREAM
1 CUP RAISINS

This is a large, tall cake. The sweet-dough crust will rise as the cake bakes, and the cake may still look a bit soft after baking, but it will set up firm as it cools — the cornstarch ensures that.

1 Preheat the oven to 375 degrees.

2 Press the cottage cheese through a sieve.

3 Combine the cornstarch and baking soda and set aside.

4 In a large mixing bowl, combine the cottage cheese with the sugar, eggs, lemon rind, and vanilla. Beat until smooth.

5 Add the dry mixture to the cheese and blend. Stir in the sour cream and raisins.

6 Pour the cheese mixture into the prepared crust and bake for 1 hour, or until done. The center will remain soft. Turn off the oven and prop the door open. Allow the cake to cool to room temperature. Serve at room temperature as well.

Greek Cheesecake

This unusual combination is less sweet than most cheesecakes. Add more honey to the batter if you find it too tart. Be sure to drain the feta and ricotta of excess liquid before blending with the rest of the ingredients.

1 Preheat the oven to 325 degrees.

2 Press the feta and ricotta cheeses through a sieve.

3 In a large mixing bowl, beat together the cheeses and honey until smooth.

4 Add the eggs, one at a time, beating thoroughly after each.

5 Pour the mixture into the prepared crust.

6 Prepare the topping. Drizzle the honey over the cake, then dust with the cinnamon.

7 Bake the cake for about 55 minutes, or until set. Cool to room temperature, then chill.

RECOMMENDATIONS:
SHORTBREAD CRUST (PAGE 50)
9-INCH SPRINGFORM PAN
HONEY TOPPING, AS GIVEN IN
RECIPE

INGREDIENTS:
½ POUND FETA CHEESE
½ POUND RICOTTA OR FARMER
CHEESE
½ POUND MILD SWISS CHEESE,
GRATED FINE
½ CUP HONEY
5 LARGE EGGS

HONEY TOPPING:
2 TABLESPOONS HONEY
1 TEASPOON GROUND
CINNAMON

Hungarian Cheesecake

RECOMMENDATIONS:
HUNGARIAN CRUST (PAGE 60)
9-INCH SPRINGFORM PAN

INGREDIENTS:
2 CUPS (1 POUND) COTTAGE
  CHEESE
4 LARGE EGGS
¼ CUP GRANULATED SUGAR
1 TEASPOON GRATED LEMON
  RIND
1 CUP SOUR CREAM
1 CUP CRUSHED PINEAPPLE,
  DRAINED
½ CUP RAISINS

Not as rich as the New World cheesecakes, perhaps, but great with a strong cup of coffee.

1 Preheat the oven to 450 degrees.

2 Press the cottage cheese through a sieve.

3 In a large mixing bowl, beat 3 eggs and the sugar until thoroughly blended.

4 Add the cottage cheese and beat, then stir in the lemon rind and the sour cream.

5 Separate the remaining egg and brush the crust with the white.

6 Combine the pineapple and raisins in a bowl, then spread the mixture evenly on the prepared crust.

7 Pour the cheese mixture on top of the pineapple-raisin mix. Bake for 10 minutes at 450 degrees, then reduce the oven temperature to 350 degrees and bake for about 35 minutes more. Cool to room temperature, then chill. Serve chilled.

Irish Curd Cake

More of a pie than a cake, this dessert has a crumbly texture and a hint of the flavor of butter.

1 Preheat the oven to 350 degrees.

2 Press the cottage cheese or curd through a sieve.

3 In a large mixing bowl, beat together the cheese, sugar, butter, lemon rind, lemon juice, and 2 egg yolks.

4 Beat the 2 egg whites until they form stiff peaks, then fold them into the cheese mixture.

5 Beat the remaining egg, then use it to paint the bottom crust to prevent sogginess.

6 Mix any remaining beaten egg with the sugar, butter, and flour to make the glaze.

7 Pour the cheese mixture into the prepared crust, then pour the glaze over the top.

8 Bake the cake for about 35 minutes, or until the top is golden. Cool to room temperature, then serve.

RECOMMENDATIONS:
SHORTBREAD CRUST (PAGE 50)
8-INCH TART PAN
SUGAR GLAZE, AS GIVEN IN
   RECIPE

INGREDIENTS:
2 CUPS (1 POUND) SWEET CURD
   OR COTTAGE CHEESE
3 TABLESPOONS GRANULATED
   SUGAR
1 TABLESPOON BUTTER,
   SOFTENED
½ TEASPOON GRATED LEMON
   RIND
½ TEASPOON LEMON JUICE
3 LARGE EGGS, 2 SEPARATED AND
   1 LEFT WHOLE

SUGAR GLAZE:
2 TABLESPOONS
   CONFECTIONERS' SUGAR
2 TABLESPOONS BUTTER,
   MELTED
2 TABLESPOONS ALL-PURPOSE
   FLOUR

Italian Cheesecake

RECOMMENDATIONS:
SHORTBREAD CRUST (PAGE 50),
   MADE WITH LEMON RIND AND
   AMARETTO LIQUEUR
9-INCH SPRINGFORM PAN

INGREDIENTS:
3¾ CUPS (30 OUNCES) RICOTTA
4 LARGE EGGS
⅔ CUP GRANULATED SUGAR
¼ CUP ALL-PURPOSE FLOUR
¼ CUP AMARETTO LIQUEUR
3 TABLESPOONS GOLDEN
   RAISINS
1 TABLESPOON FINELY CHOPPED
   CANDIED ORANGE RIND
1 TABLESPOON FINELY CHOPPED
   CANDIED LEMON RIND

Don't skip the candied rinds — they are what give this moist, soft crumbly cake its distinctive character.

1 Preheat the oven to 325 degrees.

2 Press the ricotta through a sieve.

3 In a large mixing bowl, beat together the drained cheese, eggs, sugar, and flour.

4 Stir in the liqueur, raisins, and fruits.

5 Pour the mixture into the prepared crust and bake for 1 hour. Remove the cake from the oven and cool to room temperature. Chill before serving.

New Zealand Kiwi Cheesecake

Kiwis, in case you aren't familiar with them, grow in New Zealand. They are brown and fuzzy on the outside, but once you cut them open, you reveal a gorgeous green inside. The New Zealand Kiwifruit Export Promotion Committee (yes, there is one) thinks they make a great topping for cheesecake. We agree.

1 Preheat the oven to 350 degrees.

2 In a large mixing bowl, beat together the cream cheese, milk, salt, and vanilla until thoroughly blended.

3 Add the eggs and sugar and continue to beat until light and creamy.

4 Pour the mixture into the prepared crust and bake for 35 minutes, or until lightly brown; the cake should be set in the center. Remove the cake from the oven and cool for 10 minutes.

5 Prepare the topping by mixing together the sour cream, sugar, and vanilla. Spread the topping over the top of the cake.

6 Return the cake to the oven and bake for 15 minutes more. Cool to room temperature and then refrigerate until chilled.

7 Just before serving, garnish the top of the cake with slices of kiwifruit.

RECOMMENDATIONS:
BASIC CRUMB CRUST (PAGE 46)
9-INCH SPRINGFORM PAN
KIWIFRUIT TOPPING, AS GIVEN
   IN RECIPE

INGREDIENTS:
1½ POUNDS CREAM CHEESE
2 TABLESPOONS MILK
¼ TEASPOON SALT
1 TEASPOON VANILLA EXTRACT
4 LARGE EGGS, LIGHTLY BEATEN
1 CUP GRANULATED SUGAR

KIWIFRUIT TOPPING:
1 CUP SOUR CREAM
3 TABLESPOONS
   CONFECTIONERS' SUGAR
½ TEASPOON VANILLA EXTRACT
2 KIWIS, PEELED AND SLICED

Paskha (Russian Cheesecake)

RECOMMENDATIONS:
NO CRUST
LARGE FLOWER POT, 7 × 7
   INCHES, MINIMUM
SABAYON SAUCE, AS GIVEN IN
   RECIPE

This very unusual cheesecake is a traditional Russian Easter dish. In the old days, the custom was to decorate it with paper flowers or religious emblems and have the priest come by and bless it. Back then, it was made in a special pyramid-shaped form, but you can prepare it in an ordinary red clay flower pot. Visually, the effect is quite striking, and the drainage hole allows the excess whey to escape. To make *paskha*, you'll need a large flower pot and some cheesecloth. The paskha will keep in the refrigerator for several weeks, but be sure to make it at least three days in advance.

INGREDIENTS:
6 CUPS (3 POUNDS) FARMER
   CHEESE OR LARGE-CURD
   COTTAGE CHEESE
6 EGG YOLKS
1½ CUPS CONFECTIONERS'
   SUGAR
1½ CUPS HEAVY CREAM
½ CUP CANDIED FRUITS
½ CUP SEEDLESS RAISINS
½ CUP SLIVERED ALMONDS,
   TOASTED
½ TEASPOON GRATED LEMON
   RIND
½ POUND BUTTER
3 TEASPOONS VANILLA EXTRACT

1 Press the cheese through a sieve.

2 Combine the cheese with the egg yolks, beating in 1 yolk at a time. Add the sugar and blend thoroughly.

3 Heat the cream in a large saucepan until it almost boils, then add the cheese mixture and cook over low heat, stirring constantly until the mixture thickens. Remove from the heat before it begins to boil.

4 Stir in the fruits, almonds, and lemon rind. Cool.

5 Cream together the butter and the vanilla, then stir into the cooled cheese mixture.

6 Line the flower pot with several layers of moistened cheesecloth, leaving enough cloth at the top to form a flap that will cover the pot. Fill the pot with the cheese mixture and cover with the flap. Put a weight on the top and place in the refrigerator for 2 or 3 days. The whey (liquid) will drip out the bottom of the pot, so be sure to place a pan under it.

7 When drained, carefully unmold the cake with a knife. Remove the cheesecloth and smooth the sides with a hot knife.

8 Prepare the sauce. Beat together the yolks, sugar, Madeira, and lemon rind in the top of a double boiler. Cook and continue beating until the mixture thickens.

9 Stir in the lemon juice and the rum, then chill briefly.

10 Pour the sauce over the cheesecake and serve.

SABAYON SAUCE:
2 EGG YOLKS
3 TABLESPOONS
   CONFECTIONERS' SUGAR
¼ CUP MADEIRA
½ TEASPOON GRATED LEMON
   RIND
1 TABLESPOON LEMON JUICE
1 TABLESPOON LIGHT RUM

Polish Cheesecake

RECOMMENDATIONS:
SWEET YEAST CRUST (PAGE 62)
9-INCH SPRINGFORM PAN
CRUMB TOPPING, AS GIVEN IN
   RECIPE

INGREDIENTS:
4 CUPS (2 POUNDS) DRY-CURD
   COTTAGE CHEESE OR FARMER
   CHEESE
1 TABLESPOON ALL-PURPOSE
   FLOUR
½ TEASPOON SALT
1½ CUPS GRANULATED SUGAR
4 LARGE EGGS, LIGHTLY BEATEN
½ CUP BUTTER, MELTED
1 TEASPOON VANILLA EXTRACT

CRUMB TOPPING:
1 CUP ALL-PURPOSE FLOUR
½ CUP CONFECTIONERS' SUGAR
½ TEASPOON GROUND
   CINNAMON
¼ CUP BROWN SUGAR
¼ CUP BUTTER, MELTED

Like the Czechoslovakian Cheesecake, this cake has a yeast crust, but this one also has an unusual, sweet crumb topping. The recipe comes to us courtesy of Irene Kosmalsky of Westland, Michigan, who reports that she got it from her grandmother in Poland.

1 Preheat the oven to 350 degrees.

2 Place the cottage cheese in a sieve and drain.

3 In a small bowl, mix together the flour, salt, and sugar. Set aside.

4 In a large mixing bowl, combine the cottage cheese with the eggs, butter, and vanilla. Mix together until thoroughly blended. Add the dry mixture and mix well.

5 Pour the mixture into the prepared crust and set the cake aside.

6 Prepare the topping by sifting together the flour, sugar, and cinnamon. Add the brown sugar and blend well.

7 Pour the melted butter over the topping mix and immediately stir with a fork to form small crumbs.

8 Sprinkle the topping mix over the surface of the cake and bake the cake for 50 minutes, or until done. Cool to room temperature, then chill.

Spanish Cheesecake

The cities of Spain offer pastry shops to rival the best in France. Here's a simple cake in the Spanish style.

1 Preheat the oven to 400 degrees.

2 In a large mixing bowl, cream together the cheese, 1 tablespoon butter, and sugar. Do not beat.

3 Stir in the eggs, one at a time, blending well after each.

4 Add the cinnamon, lemon rind, flour, and salt; mix well.

5 Butter the pan with the remaining 2 tablespoons butter, using your fingers to spread the butter completely.

6 Pour the mixture into the prepared pan and bake for 12 minutes at 400 degrees, then reduce the temperature to 350 degrees and bake for 25 to 30 additional minutes. The knife should come out clean. Cool the cake to room temperature, then sprinkle with confectioners' sugar.

RECOMMENDATIONS:
NO CRUST
9-INCH SPRINGFORM PAN

INGREDIENTS:
1 POUND CREAM CHEESE
3 TABLESPOONS BUTTER
1½ CUPS GRANULATED SUGAR
2 LARGE EGGS
½ TEASPOON GROUND
 CINNAMON
1 TEASPOON GRATED LEMON
 RIND
¼ CUP ALL-PURPOSE FLOUR
½ TEASPOON SALT
CONFECTIONERS' SUGAR

Swedish Cheese Pie

RECOMMENDATIONS:
BASIC PASTRY PIE CRUST
(PAGE 54), PREBAKED
9-INCH PIE PAN

INGREDIENTS:
2 CUPS (1 POUND) COTTAGE
CHEESE
3 LARGE EGGS
¼ CUP SIFTED ALL-PURPOSE
FLOUR
¼ CUP GRANULATED SUGAR
1 CUP LIGHT CREAM
⅓ CUP FINELY CHOPPED
TOASTED ALMONDS

This Scandinavian beauty isn't too sweet, but will melt in your mouth.

1 Preheat the oven to 350 degrees.

2 Press the cottage cheese through a sieve. Place in a large mixing bowl and beat until smooth.

3 Add the eggs, flour, sugar, cream, and almonds and blend well.

4 Pour the mixture into the prepared crust and bake for about 45 minutes, or until a knife comes out clean. Remove the pie from the oven and chill before serving.

Swiss Cheesecake

The unexpected flavor of swiss cheese in this light, delicate cake offers an intriguing contrast to the blander cottage cheese in it.

1 Preheat the oven to 350 degrees.

2 Press the cottage cheese through a sieve.

3 In a large mixing bowl, beat together the cottage cheese, swiss cheese, butter, flour, cornstarch, and sugar.

4 Add the egg yolks, one at a time, at a low speed, mixing thoroughly after each.

5 Beat the egg whites until they form stiff peaks, then fold into the cheese mixture.

6 Pour the mixture into the prepared crust and bake for 45 minutes. The cake will rise above the top of the pan, then settle down again. Cool in the oven with the door propped open. Chill.

RECOMMENDATIONS:
SHORTBREAD CRUST (PAGE 50)
9-INCH SPRINGFORM PAN

INGREDIENTS:
2 CUPS (1 POUND) COTTAGE CHEESE
1 CUP GRATED SWISS CHEESE
6 TABLESPOONS BUTTER, SOFTENED
3 TABLESPOONS ALL-PURPOSE FLOUR
3 TABLESPOONS CORNSTARCH
½ CUP GRANULATED SUGAR
6 EGG YOLKS
9 EGG WHITES

Ukrainian Cheesecake

RECOMMENDATIONS:
SHORTBREAD CRUST (PAGE 50)
9-INCH SPRINGFORM PAN

INGREDIENTS:
2 CUPS (1 POUND) COTTAGE
  CHFESE
3 LARGE EGGS, SEPARATED
½ CUP GRANULATED SUGAR
½ CUP SOUR CREAM
2 TEASPOONS CORNSTARCH
1 TEASPOON GRATED LEMON
  RIND
½ CUP CHOPPED WALNUTS
  (OPTIONAL)

Although typical of the cheesecakes of this region, this cake takes on an added dimension with the addition of chopped walnuts to the batter.

1 Preheat the oven to 325 degrees.

2 Press the cottage cheese through a sieve and drain.

3 In a large bowl, beat the egg yolks until light and foamy, then add the sugar slowly, continuing to beat until smooth and light.

4 Add the cottage cheese to the egg mixture, blending well, then add the sour cream, cornstarch, lemon rind, and walnuts (if desired). Stir until all ingredients are mixed completely.

5 Beat the egg whites until they form soft peaks, then gently fold them into the batter.

6 Pour the mixture into the prepared crust and bake for 1 hour. Cool to room temperature before serving.

Cheesecake Creativity

*E*nough recipes already. You'll never know the ultimate joy of cheesecake until you have invented a cheesecake of your own. It isn't nearly as difficult as it sounds. You may have to experiment a few times before you hit on the right formula, but that is part of the fun. If you have tried a few of the recipes in this book, you probably have a pretty good idea of what makes a cheesecake work. If you keep a few basic rules in mind, it should be easy to come up with a cheesecake that is just the way you want it.

As a glance through the recipes in this collection will show, there is virtually no limit to the variety of ingredients that can be used for filling or topping a cheesecake, but the best cakes seem to always have a balance of contrasting flavors and textures. A crisp crust will highlight the creamy smoothness of a well-blended custard; a few tablespoons of lemon juice will balance the sweetness of the sugar. Vanilla, almond, or other extracts will add subtlety to the blend, as will grated orange or lemon peel, used in moderation.

Probably the easiest approach is to start with a recipe that is close to what you are aiming for and then to modify it according to your taste. The richer the cheese, the richer the cheesecake, so to make a richer cake, switch from cottage cheese or neufchâtel to cream cheese. If you are already using cream cheese, increase the proportion of cream cheese to other ingredients.

Air is ultimately what makes light cheesecakes light; if you want to make a no-bake cheesecake lighter, you can do so by increasing the quantity of beaten egg whites or whipped cream, both of which contain a lot of air. Unfortunately, though, whipped cream's bubble structure won't hold up in the oven, so for baked cheesecakes, only egg whites will do.

Adding a little sugar to the egg whites once they have reached the soft-peak stage may lessen their volume slightly, but will make for a stiffer, firmer cake. For the maximum in firmness and lightness, you may want to try a technique professional bakers use. For every egg white to be beaten, set aside 4 tablespoons granulated sugar and 1 tablespoon water. Combine the sugar and water in a saucepan and heat to a temperature of 225 to 250 degrees (a candy thermometer may be helpful here). Once the whites have reached the soft-peak stage, slowly add the sugar syrup and beat until the mixture again reaches the soft-peak stage. This whole procedure must be timed carefully so that the syrup reaches the desired temperature precisely as the whites reach the soft-peak stage. If the sugar syrup heats too long, it will caramelize and burn; if the eggs sit too long, they will collapse. All in all, it is probably more bother than it is worth.

Even egg whites that are added directly to the batter will add some lightness to the blend. So for the heaviest possible cheesecake, it is best to omit the whites completely and increase the quantity of yolks appropriately.

Since egg whites and yolks harden as they bake, you can vary the firmness of a baked cheesecake by varying the quantity of these ingredients. You can also increase the firmness of a baked cake by adding flour or cornstarch, but these will also tend to make the cheesecake drier and more cakelike — which may be exactly what you want. Keep in mind that your cheesecake won't really taste cakelike unless it contains some eggs.

Since eggs don't really get a chance to set in a no-bake cheesecake, you may need to use gelatin to stiffen some of the moister no-bake batters. Here again, though, you must be careful; too much gelatin will make your cheesecake rubbery.

Once you have found a basic batter that you like, there is no end to the variety of things you can put into it or on top of it. We don't recommend anchovies, but beyond that, the possibilities are as rich as your imagination. Try a cup of your favorite fruit — fresh, canned, or candied — or a handful of chopped nut meats, or a few tablespoons of your favorite liqueur. If you use fruit or nuts in the batter, note that the cake will bake more evenly and slice more easily if the pieces are chopped fine. Nuts will add more flavor if they are toasted lightly beforehand. If you want to add flavor without changing texture, there is a wide range of spices, extracts, and essences to choose from. All the rest is up to you. Enjoy.

Index